Science and Religion in Wittgenstein's Fly-Bottle

Science and Religion in Wittgenstein's Fly-Bottle

Tim Labron

Bloomsbury Academic
An imprint of Bloomsbury Publishing Inc

B L O O M S B U R Y
NEW YORK · LONDON · OXFORD · NEW DELHI · SYDNEY

Bloomsbury Academic
An imprint of Bloomsbury Publishing Inc

1385 Broadway	50 Bedford Square
New York	London
NY 10018	WC1B 3DP
USA	UK

www.bloomsbury.com

BLOOMSBURY and the Diana logo are trademarks of Bloomsbury Publishing Plc

First published 2017

© Tim Labron, 2017

All rights reserved. No part of this publication may be reproduced or transmitted in any form or by any means, electronic or mechanical, including photocopying, recording, or any information storage or retrieval system, without prior permission in writing from the publishers.

No responsibility for loss caused to any individual or organization acting on or refraining from action as a result of the material in this publication can be accepted by Bloomsbury or the author.

Library of Congress Cataloging-in-Publication Data
A catalog record for this book is available from the Library of Congress.

ISBN: HB: 978-1-4411-1657-4
PB: 978-1-4411-5119-3
ePub: 978-1-5013-0589-4
ePDF: 978-1-5013-0590-0

Cover design: Irene Martinez Costa
Cover image © Glen Ronald

Typeset by Newgen Knowledge Works (P) Ltd., Chennai, India

To find out more about our authors and books visit www.bloomsbury.com. Here you will find extracts, author interviews, details of forthcoming events, and the option to sign up for our newsletters.

To Jacob and Kyleah

Contents

Acknowledgments   viii

1   Introduction   1
2   Philosophy and the Fly-Bottle   15
3   Physics and the Fly-Bottle   49
4   Religion and the Fly-Bottle   91
5   Conclusion   125

Bibliography   129
Index   135

Acknowledgments

I thank my publisher, Haaris Naqvi, for his professionalism and patience. I thank the Dominican and wider academic community at Blackfriars Hall (University of Oxford), along with the Centre for Studies in Religion and Society (University of Victoria), for their time and research space. Additionally, I thank Harold Coward for introducing me to the study of religion and Joshua Culling for referencing and for introducing me to the cover artist, Glen Ronald.

1

Introduction

Science and religion are key contexts for discussions of meaning and worldviews. Given the obvious influence they have, it is not surprising that questions regarding the similarities and differences between them arise. The common perspectives—for or against religion—are based on the same question: do religion and science fit together or not? Are science and religion in accord or are they diametrically opposed to each other?[1] Can a scientist also be religious? What are the values of science and religion? Are science and religion two entirely different categories without any meaningful similarity or dissimilarity?

These questions are important, and they frame the majority of discussions regarding science and religion. This frame includes ideas such as truth, objectivity, and reality; and they are typically the benchmarks of the discussion. Who, if anyone, would rather endorse ideas such as falsehood, absolute subjectivity (solipsism), and illusion? Moreover, these ideas are frequently understood through the lens of science, and in particular with the assumptions of classical physics (e.g., causality, determinism, and realism). Nonetheless, these ideas are not the objective arbitrators that define and qualify science and religion. Hence, the point of the following discussion is not to show which is closer to the above benchmarks, science or religion, but it is to show that these benchmarks can actually confuse our understanding

---

[1] I am not discussing a historical perspective on the relation between science and religion, but it is important to note Peter Harrison's remark, among others, rejecting the simple and exaggerated notion that science and religion are diametrically opposed to one another: "When examined closely, however, the historical record simply does not bear out this model of enduring warfare." *The Cambridge Companion to Science and Religion*, ed. Peter Harrison (Cambridge: Cambridge University Press, 2010), 4.

of science and religion. In general, science and religion, and our discussions of their relationship, are stuck in a fly-bottle.

A Wittgensteinian investigation can clarify science and religion on their own terms and will thereby provide a clearer discussion between them. Ludwig Wittgenstein notes: "What is your aim in philosophy?—To show the fly the way out of the fly-bottle."[2] In particular, science and religion are caught in a fly-bottle of realism—the idea that "out there" is an external reality and truth that we are discovering. Immediately, one may assume that the only alternative is therefore nonrealism. However, the following criticism of realism *does not* support nonrealism, and *does not* support the idea that there is no God. Indeed, nonrealism is equally confused as realism—the two go hand in hand. What it does support is the idea that our common conception of reality in general is a consequence of being trapped in realism and thereby distorts our discussions of science and religion.

For example, Wittgenstein obviously was never opposed to science, but he was opposed to what is now known as "scientism," namely, the belief that science, and only science, provides truth in realist terms. Religion then hastily tries to gain ground by showing that it can fall in line with the ideals of truth and realism through a comparably robust line of reasoning. Consequently, many people then consider religion to be justified if it can argue for its realist perspective. This context is most obvious in two forms of fundamentalism—religious and scientific. Certainly, the term "scientific fundamentalism" will sound odd to most since science is generally not questioned. Of course, there are many questions within science, but the pursuit and progress of science are not questioned. Nonetheless, the term is fitting since in religious and scientific forms, fundamentalism is simply two sides of the same coin rattling about in the fly-bottle.

---

[2] Ludwig Wittgenstein, *Philosophical Investigations*, trans. G. E. M. Anscombe (Oxford: Basil Blackwell, 1988), 309.

Religious fundamentalism (typically characterized as creationist) frequently mistakes a religious text as a science text. In doing this, religious fundamentalists not only confuse science, but also spend enormous amounts of time trying to justify their arguments and very little time actually coming to any deep religious understanding. This confusion is rightly criticized. However, a large number of scientists somehow escape equal criticism when they make equally confused statements regarding religion. Indeed, they also mistake a religious text as a science text! Yet in their case the "religious" text is a failed attempt at science. The general idea is that more "primitive" people did not know any better, so we need to excuse their conceptual errors as they progressed toward proper science. Certainly, Richard Dawkins rightly argues that religion is not a science, but he wrongly concludes that we should now see, given our advanced reasoning abilities, that religion is erroneous. While there may be few questions regarding his scientific work, this gloss into arguments dealing with religion is very misleading.

For example, as John Lennox says: "The idea that God and biological evolution are mutually exclusive alternatives implies first of all that God and evolution belong to the same category of explanation. But this is plainly false ... a category mistake."[3] Nonetheless, such atheistic arguments continue on the assumption that religion is nothing other than an attempt to explain things, competing with science, so as we progressively gain more and better scientific explanations we have less need, and indeed eventually no need, for religious explanations. Continuing this line of thought, Peter Atkins notes: "Science and religion cannot be reconciled, and humanity should begin to appreciate the power of its child, and to beat off all attempts at compromise. Religion has failed, and its failures should stand exposed. Science, with its currently successful pursuit of universal competence through the identification of the minimal, the supreme delight of the intellect, should be acknowledged

[3] John C. Lennox, *God's Undertaker: Has Science Buried God?* (Oxford: Liob), 89.

king."[4] Likewise, several physicists were discussing religion and God, including Werner Heisenberg, Wolfgang Pauli, and Paul Dirac, and after listening to Dirac saying things such as: "We must admit that religion is a jumble of false assertions, with no basis in reality," "primitive people," "we have no need for such solutions," Pauli subsequently remarked: "Well, our friend Dirac, too, has a religion, and its guiding principle is: 'There is no God and Dirac is His prophet.'"[5]

This process of science providing explanations where religion has failed is well known as "the god of the gaps." What is almost always missed is that this is not at all an insightful or useful point to discuss science and religion. All it does is agree that, for example, the Bible is not a science text and religion is not a science. These particular scientists show an incredible lack of understanding religion—*not* simply because they say it is false, but because of their conception of religion and the form of their arguments. Lennox rightly notes that "influential authors such as Richard Dawkins will insist on conceiving of God as an explanatory alternative to science—an idea that is nowhere to be found in theological reflection of any depth."[6] The "god of the gaps" theory seems, for these scientists, to explain the very nature of religion and exhaust its depths and still continues today.

For example, the search for the so-called god particle or the grand unified theory, according to some, clearly annihilates any belief in a god since the god theory would no longer be needed (e.g., to explain things such as gravity, time, space, subatomic particles, etc.). Lennox notes that it is confusing to think that the "concept of God, or the gods, is a placeholder for human ignorance—a 'God of the gaps', who will increasingly be displaced as the gaps in our knowledge are filled by scientific explanations, so that he will eventually disappear

---

[4] Peter W. Atkins, "The Limitless Power of Science," in *Nature's Imagination: The Frontiers of Scientific Vision*, ed. John Cornwell (Oxford: Oxford University Press, 1995), 132.
[5] Werner Heisenberg, *Physics and Beyond: Encounters and Conversations*, trans. Arnold J. Pomeranz (New York: Harper & Row, 1971), 85–7.
[6] Lennox, *God's Undertaker*, 48.

completely."[7] Does it make any sense at all to regard the discovery of a single unified theory as proof that God does not exist? Of course not. To assume it would is not all that different from thinking that dance theory is not a good explanation of the technique for winning a marathon; therefore, we no longer need dance theory. Yet, once again, religion itself is frequently stuck in the fly-bottle of realism with scientism so it, in turn, argues on the latter's terms, as noted by Henry Drummond: "Many people ceaselessly scan the fields of Nature and the books of Science in search of gaps—gaps which they fill up with God. As if God lived in the gaps? God should be sought in human knowledge, not human ignorance."[8]

The profound fundamentalism of such scientific viewpoints is startling. Again, it is not very surprising that the majority criticize religious fundamentalism, and rightly so, but that they do not as clearly criticize scientific fundamentalism should be surprising. Dawkins's arguments against religion may captivate some readers since he brings the pretext of rigorous scientific argumentation to the table, but this is clearly misleading. Perhaps Dawkins has a slight awareness of this, so he then plays the moral card and argues that religion is a greater hindrance and evil to society than the "AIDS virus, 'mad cow' disease and many others ... faith is one of the world's greatest evils, comparable to the smallpox virus but harder to eradicate."[9] Dawkins's understanding of religion and neo-Darwinianism implies that religion is similar to the caste system in classical Hindu thought, that is, there is a mechanical (at least *quasi* mechanical) reason for your current state of being. The religious person is like the outcaste. They are religious because of a glitch in their genetic makeup. They should be cast out of universities to avoid further potential contamination. Norman Malcolm rightly notes: "In our Western

---

[7] John C. Lennox, *God and Stephen Hawking: Whose Design Is It Anyway?* (Oxford: Lion Hudson, 2011), 22.
[8] Quoted in Thomas Dixon, *Science and Religion: A Very Short Introduction* (Oxford: Oxford University Press, 2008), 45.
[9] Richard Dawkins, "Is Science a Religion?," *The Humanist* (Jan.–Feb. 1997), 26.

academic philosophy, religious belief is commonly regarded as unreasonable and is viewed with condescension or even contempt. It is said that religion is a refuge for those who, because of weakness of intellect or character, are unable to confront the stern realities of the world. The objective, mature, *strong* attitude is to hold beliefs solely on the basis of evidence."[10]

The following discussion will not develop the ideas and coinage of religious or scientific fundamentalism. Indeed, religious and scientific fundamentalism trade on a hyperinflated currency with each other as they continually clink and clatter in the fly-bottle. We need to avoid this false currency and instead try to see what is really going on in religious and scientific thought. It will be shown that even if religious and scientific fundamentalism are rejected, the more thoughtful views of science and religion are also frequently stuck in the fly-bottle—but with more nuanced theories (e.g., critical realism, multiverse, etc.). To get out of this fly-bottle, as Wittgenstein understands it, means that one needs to trace their thought backward—rather than creating new theories.

It is interesting to note that the origin of this problematic fly-bottle may actually be religion. So, although the atheist scientist may consider religion to be pure nonsense, they may essentially adopt earlier religious assumptions. In other words, the above scientific view, when traced further back, has an origin in religion. Paul Davies notes:

> The orthodox concept of laws of physics derives directly from theology. It is remarkable that this view has remained largely unchallenged after 300 years of secular science. Indeed, the "theological model" of the laws of physics is so ingrained in scientific thinking that it is taken for granted. The hidden assumptions behind the concept of physical laws, and their theological provenance, are simply ignored by almost all except historians of science and theologians.[11]

---

[10] Norman Malcolm, "The Groundlessness of Belief," *Thought and Knowledge* (Ithaca, NY: Cornell University Press, 1977), 204.

[11] Paul Davies, "Universe from Bit," in *Information and the Nature of Reality: From Physics to Metaphysics*, ed. Paul Davies and Niels Henrik Gregersen (Cambridge: Cambridge University Press, 2010), 71.

Oddly, science may have ejected God, but not the metaphysical viewpoint that included God. The history of God explaining everything and having the qualities of omnipotence and omniscience shifts, for some, to science. Lennox sees this transfer in many giving science the quality of "omni-competence."[12] Not only is this transfer often missed, a subsequent and pervasive problem, in particular, is that this viewpoint goes hand in hand with a realist measuring stick that is constantly measuring and surveying the sides of the fly-bottle while there is no conception of this being the wrong measure. This will be the key running through the following discussion, namely, the problem of being stuck in the fly-bottle for science and religion is realism—even given the different subject matter of the respective disciplines. Yet, I need to continually emphasize, *this is not an argument for nonrealism, which is equally stuck in the fly-bottle.*

The problem of realism can be traced through science. For example, it can be argued that modern science, as compared to "early" science, shifts to knowledge gained through observation (empirical), and observations can accordingly confirm or falsify a theory. Galileo Galilei is certainly an example of this direction as he joins math with empirical observation. There is no question that such a perspective is very useful, but one can question to what extent it applies to our concept of reality. Galileo notes: "The great book of Nature can be read only by those who know the language in which it was written, and this language is mathematics."[13] Eventually, mathematics was seen as the perfect candidate to replace God, and particularly in theories regarding the extraordinarily small and extraordinary large. This shift has been noted by Heisenberg, who writes: "It is really possible to say ... that the nineteenth century attempted to photograph nature, while the twentieth century describes nature in a mathematical language. ... I think it would be useful to study more closely and develop this problem of parallelism between

---

[12] Lennox, *God and Stephen Hawking*, 43.
[13] Drake Stillman, *Discoveries and Opinions of Galileo* (New York: Doubleday-Anchor, 1957), 238.

science and language."[14] Heisenberg is right, and once we moved into the quantum realm, which could not be holistically pictured, but was described mathematically, the conflation of pictures with mathematics was an easy step.

Too often, mathematical axioms are thought to describe (i.e., picture) a physical object. Niels Bohr notes, regarding the calculations, that

> the entire formalism is to be considered as a tool for deriving predictions, of definite or statistical character, as regards information obtainable under experimental conditions described in classical terms and specified by means of parameters entering into the algebraic or differential equations of which the matrices or the wave functions, respectively, are solutions. These symbols themselves, as is indicated already by the use of imaginary numbers, are not susceptible to pictorial interpretation.[15]

We have too readily taken useful pictures and descriptions and then kept this perspective when moving beyond pictures and descriptions into, for example, mathematical axioms.

There are two main realist themes: one is the atomistic picture and foundationalism, that what we know can be broken down to the smallest parts, and by doing so we consequently understand reality at its foundation; the other is to extend in the opposite direction and posit ontologies of metaphysical forms or mathematics as the foundation of our reality. Even though Wittgenstein in philosophy, and Bohr and the Copenhagen interpretation in physics, have shown the problems with such views, a certain resistance is met. In the case of physics, classical physics is set in a context of cause and effect determinism; however, at the quantum level, this was obliterated. Suddenly, there

---

[14] Werner Heisenberg, Max Born, Erwin Schrodinger, and Pierre Auger, *On Modern Physics* (New York: Clarkson N. Potter, 1961), 24–5.

[15] Niels Bohr, "On the Notions of Causality and Complementarity," *Science*, 111, no. 2873 (Jan. 1950), 52.

was the problem of irreversibility, nondeterminism, the measurement problem related to the observer, the potential loss of information, etc. One result of trying to get back to the certainty of classical physics is the multiverse interpretation. According to Sean Carrol, it is a consequence of those who are concerned with the problems of the Copenhagen interpretation, and are therefore "those who think carefully about the foundations of quantum mechanics."[16] I suggest that those following his example are indeed doing a lot of thinking. The problem is that they think past the depth of the Copenhagen interpretation and return to the realist presuppositions of classical physics. Indeed, Carrol notes: "The evolution of states in quantum mechanics works just like it does in classical mechanics; it obeys a deterministic rule—the Schrodinger equation—that allows us to predict the future and past of any specific state with perfect fidelity."[17] Carrol's arguments show that the realist fly-bottle is easily continuing past classical physics—despite the clear objections of quantum theory. John Polkinghorne sees this fly-bottle when he notes: "This quantum questioning is just a particular example—in an unusually challenging one—of the fundamental philosophical debate between the realists and the positivists."[18]

The fly-bottle also applies to Wittgenstein's work. In his early work he tried to secure a foundational basis of logic for language. In a sense, the meaning of a word is determined by the object it stands for. However, he eventually saw that this was a misguided approach and turned to how we use language. Wittgenstein's point, his key point, especially in his later works, was the logic of what we *do* say; not based on logical analysis or principles such as truth functions to justify what we can and cannot say. He maintains the consistency

---

[16] Sean M. Carroll, *From Eternity to Here: The Quest for the Ultimate Theory of Time* (New York: Dutton, 2016), 240.
[17] Ibid., 249.
[18] John Polkinghorne, *Quantum Theory: A Very Short Introduction* (Oxford: Oxford University Press, 2002), 82.

of logic, but now logic is removed from a realist-type conception whereby propositions connect to external truth functions; instead, logic is seen in our propositions of mathematics, in our language. It is a problem within mathematics and physics to place an empirical logic on mathematical propositions; and in theology it is a problem to place a metaphysical logic on propositions concerning God. Wittgenstein's understanding of language will frame the way out of this problem. Moreover, as noted above, Heisenberg points out the need to investigate language and science in order to clarify our understanding of reality. This clarification is not a process of solidifying or justifying our epistemological concerns; rather, it is the logic of what we do know.

"Surely," someone may say, "look at all of the logical considerations in Wittgenstein's early work such as the *Tractatus*, we do not find that heavy handed logical account in his later works." Yet, as D. Z. Phillips notes, Rush Rhees[19] shows that Wittgenstein was continually and increasingly concerned with "showing that the questions raised in *On Certainty* [one of Wittgenstein's later works] go back as far as 1930 ... this brings out the *kind* of questions they are—that they are questions in logic, not questions in epistemology."[20] This point can easily be misunderstood by those with little knowledge of Wittgenstein's thought. Again, the point is not the principles of logic, it is logic itself. For example, is it true or false for me to say, "I live on a planet"? It is obvious that "false" is not the correct answer, but fundamentally neither is "true"! As will be discussed further in subsequent chapters, to imagine that "true" is the correct answer is to confuse logic, epistemology, and language.

---

[19] Rush Rhees was a former student and subsequent literary executor of Wittgenstein's writings. I think it is also useful to note that Rhees says he is not religious (see Rush Rhees, *Rush Rhees on Religion and Philosophy*, ed. D. Z. Phillips and Mario Von der Ruhr [Cambridge: Cambridge University Press, 1997], 202). Nonetheless, I consider his philosophy to frequently be more clarifying than many theologians.

[20] D. Z. Phillips (ed.), *Wittgenstein's on Certainty: There—Like Our Life* (Oxford: Blackwell, 2005), 135.

Thus far, mentioning things such as the problem of realism, the problem of determinism, the importance of quantum physics, Wittgenstein, Bohr, and questioning the truth condition of a proposition saying, "I live on a planet" will probably cause many questions and perhaps even worries. Bohr jarred classical physics out of its secure foundations, and Wittgenstein jarred logical positivism out of its secure foundations. In terms of theology, through a similar application, the concern will clearly be that there is a diminishing or rejection of God. However, the main reason for such concerns is directly tied to being stuck in realism and thinking that there is no other option, no exit, other than its rival nonrealism. Importantly, the realist and nonrealist see each other because they are in the same fly-bottle—while the exit is beyond both of them.

This difficulty of tracing our thought backward out of the fly-bottle is not the difficulty of creating a new theory, and definitely *not* the difficulty of finally accepting nonrealism. Rather, as Wittgenstein says:

> what makes a subject hard to understand—if it's something significant and important—is not that before you can understand it you need to be specially trained in abstruse matters, but the contrast between understanding the subject and what most people *want* to see. Because of this the very things which are most obvious may become the hardest of all to understand. What has to be overcome is a difficulty having to do with the will, rather than the intellect.[21]

Additionally, Rhees notes Wittgenstein saying: "For the scientist any suggestion of a *Betrachtung* [investigation] which abandons measurement & causality is a backsliding to something more primitive: perhaps to medicine men, and so something to be ashamed of. Or at any rate that science is the fruition of which any other view is an

---

[21] Ludwig Wittgenstein, *Culture and Value*, ed. G. H. von Wright in collaboration with Heikki Nyman, trans. Peter Winch (Chicago, IL: University of Chicago Press, 1984), 17.

inadequate anticipation *Vorstufe* [preliminary stage]."[22] We would rather progress forward on established routes or create a side path rather than go through the work and assumed regression of backtracking our thought just to check if it could lead anywhere.

Once again, despite the difficulties and potential missteps, this is a worthwhile discussion. For example, Heisenberg notes: "I believe that it is useful to let the man of science talk philosophy, and the philosopher sometimes science, even at the risk of creating new misunderstandings. The result can be so useful that it is worth running this risk."[23] Moreover, he says: "I believe that certain mistaken developments in the theory of elementary particles ... are due to the fact that their authors would claim that they do not wish to trouble about philosophy, but that in reality they unconsciously start out from a bad philosophy, and have therefore fallen through prejudice into unreasonable statements of the problem."[24] Indeed, Anton Zeilinger notes that quantum physics is in need of considerations regarding these issues: "By such a principle, I do not mean an axiomatic formalization of the mathematical foundations of quantum mechanics, but a foundational conceptual principle."[25] Furthermore, Rhees notes Wittgenstein's remark:

> But science is what scientists do. And they are not always concerned with advances in engineering. They write systematic treatises on a subject, for instance. Say a treatise on Wave Mechanics. And where the work of the scientist is concerned with what we may call clarification, philosophy may be of help to him. Though this help may not be direct,—simply the fact that a certain form of philosophical investigation is going on.[26]

---

[22] Ludwig Wittgenstein, Rush Rhees, and Gabriel Citron (eds.), "Wittgenstein's Philosophical Conversations with Rush Rhees (1939–50): From the Notes of Rush Rhees," *Mind*, 124, no. 493 (Jan. 2015), 38.
[23] Heisenberg et al., *On Modern Physics*, 32–3.
[24] Werner Heisenberg, *Tradition in Science* (New York: Seabury Press, 1983), 72.
[25] Anton Zeilinger, "A Foundational Principle for Quantum Mechanics," *Foundations of Physics*, 29, no. 4 (1999), 634.
[26] Wittgenstein et al., *Philosophical Conversations with Rush Rhees*, 36.

Wittgenstein and Bohr are arguably among the most influential figures in their respective fields. Granted, some may regard them to be infamous! They brought serious points of view to fruition and, despite their different studies, both questioned realism but neither argued for nonrealism. Given that neither conveniently fits into either category, and that most consider these to be the only two possible sides of the debate (with some variance in between, such as critical realism), it then follows that there is much confusion among interpreters. Indeed, Wittgenstein and Bohr have been described as realists by some and nonrealist by others. For example, Jim Baggot says that Bohr is a nonrealist,[27] while John Honner says he is a realist.[28] Nonetheless, Honner rightly notes that Bohr has often been wrongly labeled and tied to various philosophers to try and understand his thought;[29] however, Bohr's thought largely stands on its own. Although Honner says that Bohr is a realist, he is rightly muddled with the idea since he knows that this is not quite right.[30] Consequently, rather than seeing their insights, both Bohr and Wittgenstein were considered by many to have ventured off the path of rigorous studies and to have fallen into abstract speculations. However, I posit that this is simply a consequence of that interpreter's own realist worldview and incapability to see their insights that step out of the traditional realist view.

Once again, my point is not to prove or disprove religion, or to show that religion is respectable since it has solid arguments emulating the scientists. Rather, my point is to show how science and religion often miss their depth and continually apply their realist measuring stick to the sides of the fly-bottle while not seeing the trap. The exit can potentially be seen through Wittgenstein's clarification

---

[27] Jim Baggot, *The Quantum Story: A History in 40 Moments* (Oxford: Oxford University Press, 2011), 111.
[28] John Honner, *The Description of Nature: Niels Bohr and the Philosophy of Quantum Physics* (Oxford: Oxford University Press, 1987), 86.
[29] Ibid., 73.
[30] Ibid., 151.

of logic and language and Bohr's insights; in particular, what I call "the language matrix." This matrix represents the internal and participatory relations between language (information) and our form of life as our reality, in contrast to external categories above and beyond our domain. As Wittgenstein says: "If the place I want to get to could only be reached by way of a ladder, I would give up trying to get there. For the place I really have to get to is a place I must already be right now. Anything that I might reach by climbing a ladder does not interest me."[31]

---

[31] Wittgenstein, *Culture and Value*, 7.

2

Philosophy and the Fly-Bottle

It is useful to begin with philosophy to see how our thinking has been shaped by philosophical thought. The focus of this discussion follows the Wittgensteinian question of the relation between language and reality, and how this relation is often wrongly cast within realism. In particular, it is interesting to note the thought of René Descartes, John Locke, and George Berkeley, since it shows how realism is stuck in their thought, namely, a concern with questions such as "How do we really know things?," "How do we connect with truth?," and "How do we connect with reality?" This ties directly to Wittgenstein since his concern from the start was how language connects with reality. Is language representing a reality external to it (Locke) or is it creating reality (Berkeley)? This philosophical point, it should be clear, is analogical to the debate in physics regarding the role of the observer, and is addressed in terms of physics in the next chapter.

In the case of Wittgenstein, his early thought had close ties to realism, while his later thought does not—yet the latter does not endorse nonrealism as some may mistakenly think. Despite the fact that our understanding of reality has shifted dramatically through the advent of non-Euclidean geometry and quantum theory, I suggest that realism still has a very strong hold on our thinking, including Wittgenstein's early thought. The following is certainly not a history of realism, nor a comprehensive overview; rather, selected points are taken to provide a basic understanding of realism in order to better understand the move out of realism.

Descartes's title as "the father of modern philosophy" is well known. For our purpose, it is important to see how his influential thinking shaped our current thought. Generally speaking, Descartes places a distance between the individual and the external world in which that figure resides. This distance is an epistemological distance; that is, as the individual moves from the private to the external, epistemological certainly diminishes. Given the separation of an external reality and the human being, it was a natural consequence to have subsequent thinkers attempt to ease the problematic gap and the resultant skepticism opened by Descartes. This separation has the mark of realism, that is, reality is external to us and we do our best to work out how we have knowledge of it. This is a fly-bottle constructed out of realism and skepticism.

Descartes's subsequent search for certainty leads him to require that every assertion be based on a proof, and that no proof will be based on weak assumptions. He states: "The senses deceive, and it is prudent never to trust completely those who have deceived us even once."[1] Indeed, Descartes regards the basis of knowledge up to his day to be very weak and he thereby rejects everything—he doubts everything. He notes: "Regarding philosophy, I shall say only this: seeing that it has been cultivated for many centuries by the most excellent minds and yet there is still no point in it which is not disputed and hence doubtful."[2] So how does Descartes proceed to gain knowledge, now that he has doubted everything? He begins with reason alone; in other words, knowledge derived from the senses is something that one can doubt. In his reduction from the senses to reason, he eventually comes to the conclusion: *cogito, ergo Sum*, that is, "I am thinking, therefore I exist." In other words, he cannot doubt doubt. This is the foundation on which Descartes creates the building plan for his

---

[1] René Descartes, *The Philosophical Writings of Descartes*, trans. J. Cottingham, R. Stoothoff, and D. Murdoch (Cambridge: Cambridge University Press, 1985), 2:12.
[2] Ibid., 1:114–15.

structure of knowledge. This building plan calls for what Descartes names the "clear and distinct" rule. In other words, the senses are left aside while the planning begins with that which can be intuited. He says:

> By "intuition" I do not mean the fluctuating testimony of the sense or the deceptive judgement of the imagination as it botches things together, but the conception of a clear and attentive mind, which is so easy and distinct that there can be no room for doubt about what we are understanding... intuition is the indubitable conception of a clear and attentive mind which proceeds solely from the light of reason ... thus everyone can mentally intuit that he exists, that he is thinking, that a triangle is bounded by just three sides and a sphere is a single surface, and the like.[3]

There is, of course, a foundation for the "intuition" planning. It is the *lux naturae* and the guarantee of a truthful and honest God.

It follows that Descartes views the separation between the mind and physical reality as a dualistic relation. He can doubt that he has a body, but he cannot doubt that he has a mind. He writes: "This 'I' ... is entirely distinct from the body, and indeed is easier to know than the body, and would not fail to be whatever it is, even if the body did not exist."[4] The separation that Descartes makes between the mind and the body creates an uncrossable bridge, and seeing this difficulty Descartes assumes that a pineal gland in one's brain must be the nexus between the body and the mind. Yet this mysterious body part is nothing more than a Band-Aid on an amputation. The material world is amputated and it is cut off from the mind. Consequently, reality and knowledge are sought and founded on an abstract, and perhaps unreal, intellectual realm. The epistemological problems that Descartes set led others on the search for better ways to secure knowledge, as is found in the realism of Locke and the idealism of Berkeley.

[3] Ibid., 1:14.
[4] Ibid., 1:27.

Locke continues Descartes's separation between our ideas and the external world, but unlike Descartes, he regards the senses as somewhat reliable. While Descartes created an abyss between the individual and the external world in terms of knowledge, Locke specifies a distance between the individual and the substance of the world and consequently creates differing qualities that, to a certain extent, connect the individual and these substances.

Locke writes:

> It is an established opinion amongst men that there are in the understanding certain innate principles, some primary notions ... characters as it were stamped upon the mind of man, which the soul receives at its very first being, and brings into the world with it. It would be sufficient to convince unprejudiced readers of the falseness of this supposition if I could only show (as I hope I shall in the following parts of this Discourse) how men ... may attain to all the knowledge they have without the help of any innate impressions.[5]

Rather than a library of innate ideas, Locke considers the "intellect" to be essentially empty shelving unless we have sense impressions and gain knowledge through experience.[6] Of course, Locke is not suggesting that reality is a direct mirror representation of the senses (naive realism); instead, he suggests that in terms of realism there is a real world "out there" and our sense perceptions cause mental events. This is a causal process whereby through experience one gains ideas that are the books to fill the library shelves. This form of gaining knowledge is a type of atomism since the primary building block is the simplest perceptual unit (simple ideas), which then combine to form a compound of these ideas. For instance, we have the perceptual unit of red, a geodesic shape, etc., and then eventually end up with an apple. The search for reality leads Locke to realism,

---

[5] John Locke, *An Essay Concerning Human Understanding*, ed. with a foreword by Peter H. Nidditch (Oxford: Clarendon Press, 1985), 48.
[6] Ibid., 104.

and the idea that our senses can provide us with some knowledge of the real world.

The empiricism that Locke presents is based on two distinct qualities: primary and secondary. The former qualities are held by the object itself while the latter are in the mind. Thus, what we measure, such as geometric shape, length, etc., are primary; while what we perceive is secondary. When we see a red apple the color is not in the object itself; instead, it is a reflection off the object. It then follows, for Locke, that we are never able to fully know or perceive physical reality, only representations of it. Locke notes that the mind "perceives nothing but its own *ideas*."[7] Although Descartes is typically labeled a rationalist and Locke an empiricist, and contra-Descartes, Locke regards the physical world as an independent reality and the source of our ideas and knowledge, Locke nonetheless maintains the Cartesian separation between ideas (our mind) and the physical world, but now with the Band-Aid of various qualities.

Berkeley agrees with Descartes and Locke that we have immediate experience only of our own ideas. However, he sees the problem of skepticism that both Descartes and Locke thereby fall into—given the distance from one's ideas to the physical world. Therefore, in order to maintain the central point of the mind and ideas, yet negate the problematic skepticism regarding the external world, he solves the problem by rejecting the external world. If there is no independent external world, then there is nothing to be skeptical about!

The skeptic questions whether or not, and if so how, the external world connects to our knowledge of it; alternatively, perhaps the world is a human creation. Locke thinks that our ideas, as best as is possible, mirror the external world (realism) while Berkeley thinks that the world mirrors our ideas (idealism). Berkeley notes: "Let anyone consider those arguments, which are thought manifestly to prove that colours and tastes exist only in the mind, and he shall find they

[7] Ibid., 583.

may, with equal force, be brought to prove the same thing of extension, figure and motion."[8] Berkeley sees the trouble with empiricism, and thereby jumps to a seemingly opposite direction, namely, idealism. Essentially, Berkeley entirely removes the distance between the assumed external world and the individual by "simply" placing it in the individual's mind. This is, in a sense, taking Locke's idea to the extreme. Since Locke considers the mind to only "really" perceive its own ideas, it then follows, for Berkeley, that that is all we have—our ideas. However, Berkeley is not outside of the realism fly-bottle. His arguments are directly related to realism. In other words, he begins with realism and then comes up with a new theory given these arguments. What is needed, however, is not a new theory within the fly-bottle, but a dissolving of the fly-bottle.

Wittgenstein provides an illuminating exit from realism, and in order to show this it is useful to first discuss his early realist tendencies. Rather than deleting an external reality outside one's mind, Wittgenstein continues the realist question of how there is a link with an external reality. In particular, he investigates how language connects with reality. Likewise, Locke remarks:

> Words, as they are used by Men, can properly and immediately signify nothing but the *Ideas* that are in the Mind of the speaker; yet they in their thoughts give them secret reference to two other things. First, they suppose their Words to be marks of the Ideas in the Minds also of other Men ... Secondly ... they often suppose their Words to stand also for the reality of things.[9]

In other words, for Locke the immediate signification for words is a private idea that is separated by various qualities from actual reality; however, an actual reality must be "out there" to avoid both the extreme view of Berkeley and any notion of complete arbitrariness.

---

[8] George Berkeley, *A Treatise Concerning the Principles of Human Knowledge*, ed. with an introduction by G. J. Warnock (La Salle, IL: Open Court, 1962), 302.

[9] Locke, *Concerning Human Understanding*, 406–7.

Likewise, Wittgenstein was always concerned with how language connects to reality.

In Wittgenstein's early work the elements of realism, and indeed elements of a Platonic realism in his logical form, point toward the independence and uniformity of nature that our knowledge and language reflect. This entails in realist fashion that knowledge and language are in an external and independent relation to that reality. For Locke there must be a uniformity of nature and for Wittgenstein, in particular, a uniform logic. Wittgenstein uses a picture theory of meaning to point out what we *can* say in contrast to what we *cannot* say. We can picture a possible or an actual state of affairs in the world. One clear example used by Wittgenstein is hieroglyphic writing, "which pictures the facts it describes."[10] A hieroglyph pictures something in the world and, according to Wittgenstein, a proposition also pictures something in the world and is "a picture of reality."[11] Hence, the proposition is a logical construction of possible states in the world and can be verified as true or false by comparing the picture (proposition) with reality. If the proposition can be said and has sense, then there is a link with reality. Granted, even if a proposition has sense it may be false. For example, the proposition "I am now typing and my computer is on top of my desk" is true; however, there is sense in me saying, "I am typing and my computer is under my desk," although this is false. The point here is that propositions must make sense and must be either true or false. This is, of course, in contrast to nonsense, such as "my desk is a thirsty ruler."

Yet Wittgenstein noticed that the above ordinary language can be reduced further. The proposition can be reduced to elementary propositions. While Locke was busy sorting out qualities to try and understand the relation to reality, Wittgenstein was reducing language from

---

[10] Ludwig Wittgenstein, *Tractatus Logico-Philosophicus*, trans. Raymond Hargreaves and Roger White (London: Routledge & Kegan Paul, 1986), 4.016.
[11] Ibid., 4.01.

a proposition picturing reality to its basic building blocks. The elementary proposition can be reduced to names, which then connect with reality, and so connected "a name means an object. The object is its meaning."[12] That is, the name stands in for a simple object in the world. So, although a proposition can be false, there are no false names (no false reality). The name and the simple object for which it stands are the contact with reality (e.g., the world). It should be clear that the word "computer" does not name a simple object; it can be reduced from composite ordinary language through logical analysis toward a name and a simple object. The computer can be broken down to a processor, etc., describing the relation to reality through this reduction. However, this reduction is unsurprisingly difficult, and Wittgenstein never gave an example of a simple object or name. Nonetheless, he notes: "It does not go against our feeling, that *we* cannot analyse propositions so far to mention the elements by name; no, we feel that the world must consist of these elements."[13] In order to ensure stability and uniformity and to avoid an infinite regress, Wittgenstein assumes that there must be simple objects and names that connect with reality in order to build propositions. So, there is, according to Wittgenstein, a limit, and this limit is the possible configurations of simple objects and their constitutive names. This is the limit of what can possibly be said. Wittgenstein, in line with realism and the empiricist understanding of language, regards language as linking with an external reality. There is a separation between human contexts and the sense of a proposition requiring a causal process from the proposition down to its logical syntax. That is, the projective relation is the meaning.

Through the *Tractatus* Wittgenstein sought, in line with classical physics, to provide an analysis and description of the nature of the

---

[12] Ibid., 3.203.
[13] Ludwig Wittgenstein, *Notebooks*, ed. G. H. von Wright and G. E. M. Anscombe, trans. G. E. M. Anscombe (Oxford: Blackwell, 1979), 62.

world—how it really is as we reflect its reality. As discussed in the following chapter, it is interesting to note that Wittgenstein's requirement of a simple object has some similarities to thinking that there is an isomorphic relation between the simplest elements and our pictures, which is also necessary for the understanding of many physicists of his time (e.g., Ludwig Boltzmann), to determine the meaning of propositions or to determine the "machine" account of physics.

It is important to note, however, that Wittgenstein was not simply a logical positivist, as Paul Engelmann rightly notes:

> A whole generation of disciples was able to take Wittgenstein for a positivist because he has something of enormous importance in common with the positivists: he draws the line between what we can speak about and what we must be silent about just as they do. The difference is only that they have nothing to be silent about. Positivism holds—and this is its essence—that what we can speak about is all that matters in life. *Whereas Wittgenstein passionately believes that all that really matters in human life is precisely what, in his view, we must be silent about.* When he nevertheless takes immense pains to delimit the unimportant, it is not the coastline of that island which he is bent on surveying with such meticulous accuracy, but the boundary of the ocean.[14]

That which Wittgenstein regards as significant beyond the boundaries are, for example, ethics, value, logical form, and religion.

The importance that Wittgenstein places on what cannot be said, including logical form, is addressed later. In short, although propositions connect to an external reality and have a common structure to that external reality, that there is this structure cannot be explained with propositions since to do so one would need to move outside this relationship. Instead, there is an established harmony that cannot be said but is shown in the proposition, and Wittgenstein calls this

---

[14] Paul Engelmann, *Letters from Ludwig Wittgenstein, with a Memoir*, ed. B. F. McGuiness, trans. L. Furtmuller (Oxford: Basil Blackwell, 1967), 143–4.

logical form, and it has an a priori status as that to which language connects (realism), and thereby invites a comparison between his simple objects and Platonic Forms.

Granted, Wittgenstein's simple objects and the Platonic Forms remain rather elusive, and are more theoretical than substantial. Yet Descartes separates the mind from the physical world, Locke separates ideas from substance, and Wittgenstein separates logic from human convention. Certainly, Descartes's *cogito, ergo sum*, Locke's "unknown something," Berkeley's mind, the Platonic Forms, and Wittgenstein's simple object are very different from one another, yet they are all maintained as metaphysical foundations and primary, while human convention is secondary as it connects to these external realities. In the *Tractatus* Wittgenstein provides a description of how using a sign logically, that is, how logical form gives meaning to signs, is the connection between language and an independent reality.

Although Wittgenstein's early thought held aspects of realism, his later thought does not. Indeed, Wittgenstein himself says that there was a shift in his thought: "It suddenly seemed to me that I should publish those old thoughts and the new ones together: that the latter could be seen in the right light only by contrast with and against the background of my old way of thinking."[15] Wittgenstein's Tractarian "old" thought held a type of atomism, whereby truth and falsity systematically lead to a complete analysis to determine what is or is not a true or false proposition. As Wittgenstein notes regarding his "old" thought: "There seemed to pertain to logic a peculiar depth—a universal significance. Logic lay, it seemed, at the bottom of all the sciences.—For logical investigation explores the nature of all things. It seeks to see the bottom of all things and is not meant to concern itself whether what actually happens is this or that."[16] However, his later thought regards this focus on such a logic, and regarding propositions

---

[15] Wittgenstein, *Philosophical Investigations*, viii.
[16] Ibid., §89.

to necessarily be true or false, to be misleading since it dismisses (to some extent) the actual use of propositions and leaves truth and falsity to determine what can or cannot be a proposition. He writes:

> Formerly, I myself spoke of a "complete analysis", and I used to believe that philosophy had to give a definite dissection of propositions so as to set out clearly all their connections and remove all possibility of a misunderstanding. I spoke as if there were a calculus in which such a dissection would be possible ... At the root of all this there was a false and idealized picture of the use of language.[17]

What is happening is that Wittgenstein no longer tries to bridge the gap between the external world and language by means of the Tractarian independent true or false elementary propositions; instead, propositions are internally related and show the logic they have in their use—logic does not underlie propositions as an external foundation.

This is a further rejection of Logical Positivism as he moves away from truth functions of elementary propositions to explain language, toward describing the use of language. Peter Winch rightly notes that there are, of course, certain limits on propositions, what we can say, and we are thereby

> limited by certain formal requirements centering around the demand for consistency. But these formal requirements tell us nothing about what in particular is to *count* as consistency, just as the rules of the predicate calculus limit but do not determine what are to be the proper values of p, q, etc. We can only determine this by investigating the wider context of the life in which the activities in question are carried on.[18]

In other words, we do not simply have a single proposition that is formed by the building blocks of names and elementary propositions and then

---

[17] Ludwig Wittgenstein, *Philosophical Grammar*, ed. Rush Rhees, trans. Anthony Kenny (Oxford: Basil Blackwell, 1974), 211.
[18] Peter Winch, *Ethics and Action* (London: Routledge & Kegan Paul, 1972), 35.

build a system; instead, we start with a system of propositions.[19] As Wittgenstein notes, "Philosophy is not laid down in sentences, but in language."[20] For Wittgenstein there is no longer a foundational underlying structure of simple objects on which language depends for uniformity; now unity is found in the use of language, still a logical form, but it is "in" the use of language, not external to language.

Wittgenstein then rejects the idea that there are simple objects on which we eventually build language, as if there is, as Bertrand Russell says, the "ultimate furniture of the world."[21] In contrast to his earlier thought, Wittgenstein now makes it clear that there is no a priori external foundation that underlies language: "The grammar of a language isn't recorded and doesn't come into existence until language has already been spoken by human beings for a *long* time. Similarly, primitive games are played without their rules being codified, and even without a single rule being formulated."[22] Human activity and choice, in what Wittgenstein calls the form of life, becomes his focus rather than an underlying logical form. This does not mean that there is no logic; rather, it means that the logic is formed and seen in the form of life. He notes: "The rules of grammar are arbitrary in the same sense as the choice of a unit of measurement. But that means no more than that the choice is independent of the length of the objects to be measured and that the choice of one unit is not 'true' and another 'false' in the way that a statement of length is true or false."[23] Humans choose what unit of measurement to use and "exactness" is not something shown by means of something outside our language and everyday conversations.

---

[19] Ludwig Wittgenstein, *On Certainty*, ed. G. E. M. Anscombe and G. H. von Wright, trans. Denis Paul and G. E. M. Anscombe (Oxford: Basil Blackwell, 1979), 105.
[20] Ludwig Wittgenstein, "Sections 86–93 (pp. 405–35) of the So-Called 'Big Typescript,'" ed. Heikki Nyman, trans. C. G. Luckhardt and M. A. E. Aue, *Synthese*, 87, no. 1 (Apr. 1991), 6.
[21] Bertrand Russell, *Introduction to Mathematical Philosophy* (Russell House: Spokesman, 2008), 182.
[22] Wittgenstein, *Philosophical Grammar*, 62–3.
[23] Ibid., 185.

Wittgenstein rightly says: "Giving grounds, however justifying the evidence, comes to an end;—but the end is not certain propositions striking us immediately as true, i.e. it is not a kind of *seeing* on our part; it is our *acting* which lies at the bottom of the language-game."[24] The acting and using of language lead to his idea of the language-game, as he says: "The term 'language-*game*' is meant to bring into prominence the fact that the speaking of a language is part of an activity or a form of life."[25] Wittgenstein no longer places logic as something that language must connect with; instead, it is shown in the applications of language. He notes: "Children do not learn that books exist, that armchairs exist, etc., etc.,—they learn to fetch books, sit in arm chairs, etc., etc."[26] In other words: "It is part of the grammar of the word 'chair' that this is what we call 'to sit in a chair.'"[27]

It follows that a confusion in language is not the result of a wrong connection to any underlying structure; rather, it is a confusion regarding the actual use of language in our form of life. In other words, confusion is not the result of wrongly connecting to external strictures, such as an independent logical syntax, but it is the problem of using language outside its particular language-game. Wittgenstein remarks: "It is interesting to compare the multiplicity of the tools in language and of the ways they are used, the multiplicity of kinds of word and sentence, with what logicians have said about the structure of language. (Including the author of the *Tractatus Logico-Philosophicus*.)"[28] Instead of a strict logical analysis based on logical principles, Wittgenstein says: "Our language can be seen as an ancient city: a maze of little streets and squares, of old and new houses, and of houses with additions from various periods; and this surrounded by a multitude of new boroughs with straight regular streets and uniform

---

[24] Wittgenstein, *On Certainty*, 204.
[25] Wittgenstein, *Philosophical Investigations*, §23.
[26] Wittgenstein, *On Certainty*, 476.
[27] Ludwig Wittgenstein, *The Blue and Brown Books* (Oxford: Basil Blackwell, 1972), 24.
[28] Wittgenstein, *Philosophical Investigations*, §23.

houses."²⁹ Peter Winch also notes this point: "The criteria of logic are not a direct gift of God, but arise out of, and are only intelligible in the context of, ways of living and modes of social life."³⁰ Moreover, İlhamn Dilman aptly remarks:

> While in the *Tractatus* logic does not need and does not have any metaphysical foundations in an independent reality—"logic must look after itself"—it is itself a metaphysical foundation of natural languages. Actual languages conform to it; they are the tail which logic with a capital L, as top dog, wags. In the *Investigations* this relation is reversed and the capital L is dropped from both logic and language. We have "language-games" which are themselves part of human life ... Logic appears in that. It does not have an independent anchor outside or separate from our natural languages and the language-games which form part of such languages ... Thus logic, although its principles, like the positions of mathematics, are timelessly true, it is not itself rooted in anything timeless.³¹

Wittgenstein moves away from separating language and reality, and thereby also removes the epistemological fallout of maintaining such a separation.

Wittgenstein is not interested in how we can explain and determine what we can know and say; now he is interested in what we do know and say. He writes: "All testing, all confirmation and dis-confirmation of a hypothesis takes place already within a system. And this system is not a more or less arbitrary and doubtful point of departure for all our arguments; no, it belongs to the essence of what we call an argument. The system is not so much the point of departure, as the element in which arguments have their life."³² Moreover, he notes:

> The stream of life, or the stream of the world, flows on and our propositions are only verified by the present. And so in some way they must

---

²⁹ Ibid., §18.
³⁰ Peter Winch, *The Idea of a Social Science* (London: Routledge & Kegan Paul, 1958), 100–1.
³¹ İlham Dilman, *Wittgenstein's Copernican Revolution* (New York: Palgrave, 2002), 27.
³² Wittgenstein, *On Certainty*, 105.

be commensurable with the present; and they cannot be so *in spite of* their spatio-temporal nature; on the contrary this must be related to their commensurability as the corporeality of a ruler to its being extended—which is what enables it to measure.[33]

Thus, the way out of confusion is not to develop further metaphysical theories, but to pay attention to the way language is used in context. He writes: "When philosophers use a word—'knowledge', 'being' ... and try to grasp the essence of a thing, one must always ask oneself; is the word actually used in this way in the language-game which is its original home?—What *we* do is to bring words back from their metaphysical to their everyday use."[34] Wittgenstein thereby rejects realism and epistemology: "Why should the language-game rest on some kind of knowledge?"[35]

Wittgenstein noted that philosophers "constantly see the method of science before their eyes, and are irresistibly tempted to ask and answer questions in the way science does. This tendency is the real source of metaphysics, and leads the philosopher into complete darkness. I want to say here that it can never be our job ... to explain anything. Philosophy really is purely descriptive."[36] Language is not composed of various isolated points; rather, it is an interrelated system that forms through human activity and use in our form of life. We are not simply solitary observers or secondarily relying on a primary external foundation. The result is that, for Wittgenstein, metaphysics and skepticism lose their significance since there are no links to be made to an external reality to guarantee meaning and knowledge. He does this neither by providing better theories to link to an external reality nor by denying an external reality; instead, he rejects misleading theories that assume various connections to an external

---

[33] Ludwig Wittgenstein, *Philosophical Remarks*, ed. Rush Rhees, trans. Raymond Hargreaves and Roger White (Oxford: Basil Blackwell, 1975), 81.
[34] Wittgenstein, *Philosophical Investigations*, §116.
[35] Wittgenstein, *On Certainty*, 477.
[36] Wittgenstein, *Blue and Brown Books*, 18.

reality. What determines a proposition is not the underlying logic or the ontological forms above it, but, as Wittgenstein sees, the movement and relationships between propositions. Our contact with reality is certainly mediated through language, yet that reality is neither reduced to language nor independent of it.

This rejection of an external foundation that we build on leaves some individuals fearing arbitrariness; however, this is a direct consequence of missing the significance of the form of life. Wittgenstein anticipates this difficulty, so he notes: "'So are you saying that human agreement decides what is true and what is false?' It is what human beings say that is true and false; and they agree in the language they use. That is not agreement in opinions but in the form of life."[37] We do not simply receive data as passive observers (against realism) and we do not simply make whatever we want out of the data (idealism). Furthermore, Wittgenstein remarks:

> If a proposition too is conceived as a picture of a possible state of affairs and is said to show the possibility of the state of affairs, still the most that the proposition can do is what a painting or relief of film does: and so it can at any rate not set forth what is not the case. So does it depend wholly on our grammar what will be called (logically) possible and what not,—i.e. what the grammar permits?—But surely that is arbitrary!—Is it arbitrary?—It is not every sentence-like formation that we know how to do something with, not every technique has an application in our life; and when we are tempted in philosophy to count some quite useless thing as a proposition, that is often because we have not considered its application sufficiently.[38]

That a chair does exist is taken for granted, and it is within our use of the chair that our propositions show that we know the meaning of a chair, but whether there are two or more chairs in the room is independent of language. As Dilman notes: "What language is used to

---

[37] Wittgenstein, *Philosophical Investigations*, §241.
[38] Ibid., §520.

refer to, speak about, describe or state is independent of the language in the sense that what we say in it can be false; saying it does not make it true. But the grammatical dimension within which we speak, say something true or false, is internal to the language."[39] Wittgenstein's point may wrongly appear to be not only inviting relativism, but also rather underwhelming, and unimportant. Yet he says: "Where does our investigation get its importance from, since it seems to only destroy everything interesting, that is, all that is great and important? (As it were all the buildings, leaving behind only bits of stone and rubble.) What we are destroying is nothing but houses of cards and we are clearing up the ground of language on which they stand."[40] Formerly, Wittgenstein says the philosopher's task is to "give meaning to certain signs in his propositions";[41] later he says, once again: "What is your aim in philosophy?—To show the fly the way out of the fly-bottle."[42] The way out is not by creating a new theory or explanation, it is by means of dissolving the confusion itself. Moreover, what is rejected is skepticism since there is nothing to be skeptical about in terms of language being connected to an external reality since the grammatical rules are internal to language. In other words, Wittgenstein shifts from the external underlying logical syntax of language, which is an external logical form that language connects to or mirrors, to logical form being shown in the language we use and the many internal connects between language-games—this is the logic of what we do say, not the epistemology of how we know that language connects to an external independent reality.

This understanding of language and reality follows through to Wittgenstein's understanding of mathematics. Like Wittgenstein's early thought, there is generally a drive in mathematics to reduce complexity to more simple formulas, and eventually to the Theory of

[39] Dilman, *Wittgenstein's Copernican Revolution*, 34.
[40] Wittgenstein, *Philosophical Investigations*, §118.
[41] Wittgenstein, *Tractatus Logico-Philosophicus*, 6.53.
[42] Wittgenstein, *Philosophical Investigations*, §309.

Everything.⁴³ For example, David Hilbert thought that mathematics could be "reduced to a set of written marks that could be manipulated according to prescribed rules without any attention being paid to the applications that would give 'significance' to those marks."⁴⁴ However, Kurt Godel's incompleteness theorems proved that in mathematics the whole is greater than the sum of the parts. Thus, there is a limit to reductionism. Moreover, as noted by Lennox, it follows that "Peter Atkins' statement ... that 'the only grounds for supposing that reductionism will fail are pessimism in the minds of the scientists and fear in the minds of the religious' is simply incorrect."⁴⁵

There is some similarity between questioning the connection between language and reality and that between mathematics and reality. In the earlier discussion it was noted that the Cartesian turn of separating the individual from an external reality leads, in part, to epistemological theories ranging from idealism to empiricism. Wittgenstein was arguing, as S. G. Shanker says, against the "Cartesian tradition of trying to resolve these problems [of mathematical truth] epistemologically."⁴⁶ As noted by Stig Stenholm, this pattern is found in mathematics: "'Formalism' versus 'contentful mathematics' is like idealism versus realism. It will become obsolete in that each party makes unjust assertions at variance with the day-to-day practice."⁴⁷ Whether the focus is idealism or realism, or formalism versus contentful mathematics, the problem is the same, namely, seeking a justification for language in one case and mathematics in the other. The reason there is a search for justification is the assumption that skepticism is always lurking around the corner given the distance between us, our language, and the real truth—or, in short, realism.

---

⁴³ Lennox, *God's Undertaker*, 52.
⁴⁴ Ibid., 52.
⁴⁵ Ibid., 53.
⁴⁶ S. G. Shanker, *Wittgenstein and the Turning-Point in the Philosophy of Mathematics* (New York: State University of New York, 1987), 26.
⁴⁷ Stig Stenholm, *The Quest for Reality: Bohr and Wittgenstein* (New York: Oxford University Press), 179.

Clearly, mathematics has been and is still viewed by many as the mainstay of truth and reality in contrast to other disciplines. Surely we can say that 2 + 2 = 4 is certain and that no doubt can find any foothold. For example, as Shanker notes, "Newton's *Principia* descended on a culture which, because it believed that 'the universe is mathematical in structure and behaviour, and nature acts in accordance with inexorable and immutable laws', was predisposed to accept that Newton had successfully penetrated its veil."[48] We assume that mathematical symbols must refer to reality, and therefore mathematics must be about true mathematical objects. Additionally, Roger Penrose notes: "The world of perfect forms is primary ... its existence being almost a logical necessity—and ... the world of conscious perceptions and the world of physical reality are its shadows."[49] An alternate view is offered by Bertrand Russell, yet it also seeks a foundation outside our everyday lives. He notes: "Mathematics takes us still further from what is human, into the region of absolute necessity, to which not only the actual world, but every possible world, must conform."[50] Russell, rather than looking for abstract entities in the heavens, sought a logical foundation of mathematics; and we are reminded of Wittgenstein's Tractarian comment: "Language disguises thought; so that from the external form of the clothes one cannot infer the form of thought they clothe, because the external form of the clothes is constructed with quite another object than to let the body be recognized."[51] These thoughts vary significantly from one another, yet they all have a tendency to abstract language and mathematics from our ordinary language and forms of life in favor of a foundation, that is, behind a veil, beyond the shadow of the world, and not of the actual world.

---

[48] Shanker, *Wittgenstein and the Turning-Point*, 269.
[49] Roger Penrose, *Shadows of the Mind: A Search for the Missing Science of Consciousness* (Oxford: Oxford University Press, 1994), 417.
[50] Bertrand Russell, *The Basic Writings of Bertrand Russell*, ed. E. Egner and Lester E. Dennon (New York: Routledge, 2009), 229.
[51] Wittgenstein, *Tractatus Logico-Philosophicus*, 4.002.

As previously mentioned, it is interesting to note how God was incorporated in philosophy and mathematics at an early stage where, for example, God was a guarantor of meaning and uniformity. God was, in part, a foundational principle. Even more recently Georg Cantor not only thought that there is an actual infinite, but also remarked: "From me, Christian philosophy will be offered for the first time the true theory of the infinite."[52] God has now largely been dropped out of the thought of most philosophers and mathematicians, yet the function of God as a foundational principle often remains, but now rather than an external and independent God there is an external and independent foundation of, for example, metaphysics, logical atomism, or mathematics.

From Pythagoras saying "all is number" to current theories today, an extreme form of regarding mathematics as our reality is found in Max Tegmark's work, where he wants to reject all "human baggage" and concepts in order to describe the basis of all reality—a completely unconditional reality, namely, mathematics. He rightly sees that this entails relations (between numbers), but wrongly thinks that this mathematical structure *is* reality. He calls this the "Mathematical Universe Hypothesis" and notes: "If we assume that reality exists independently of humans, then for a description to be complete, it must also be well defined according to nonhuman entities—aliens or supercomputers, say—that lack any understanding of human concepts."[53] This is an extreme form of realism based on a Platonist conception of an object reality that is numerical and absolutely independent. Norman Malcolm's remark is not directed toward Tegmark, yet it is apt:

> It is as if this certainty is so powerful that not even God could so manage things as to make it doubtful. Wittgenstein hits the nail on the head with his remark, "Is God bound by our knowledge: are a lot of our statements incapable of falsehood?" ... In Descartes's theory it is

---

[52] Joeseph Dauben, *Georg Cantor: His Mathematics and Philosophy of the Infinite* (Princeton, NJ: Princeton University Press, 1990), 147.
[53] Max Tegmark, *Our Mathematical Universe: My Quest for the Ultimate Nature of Reality* (New York: Knopf, 2014), 255.

explicit that God is bound by our clear and distinct perceptions: for His making them false would be a contradiction of His essential veracity, and so is impossible.[54]

Of course, Tegmark does not posit God as a foundation, but he functions within a parallel conception.

Likewise, when Albert Einstein famously says that "God does not play dice," he is not invoking or necessarily believing that there is a God who does not play dice; rather, he is saying that reality is independent and determined. Indeed, if there was a God, then this God would be caught in Malcolm's noted contradiction.

Given this conception of mathematics, Wittgenstein starkly notes:

> The comparison with alchemy suggests itself. We might speak of a kind of alchemy in mathematics. Is it the earmark of this mathematical alchemy that mathematical propositions are regarded as statements about mathematical objects,—and so mathematics as the exploration of these objects. In a certain sense it is not possible to appeal to the meaning of the signs in mathematics, just because it is only mathematics that gives them their meaning.[55]

To assume that numbers exist somewhere beyond us to determine our calculations, or that logic or simple objects underlie mathematics and language to determine what we can and cannot say, and how we calculate, is upside down. Or, more properly, not even upside down since not only are these structures a confusion, but also the logic in language and mathematics is internal to their respective propositions. Mathematics does not arise from numbers, mathematics gives numbers meaning; and language does not arise from logic, it is in language that we understand logic and by calculating that we understand numbers.

---

[54] Norman Malcolm, *Nothing Is Hidden: Wittgenstein's Criticism of His Early Thought* (Oxford: Basil Blackwell, 1986), 224.

[55] Ludwig Wittgenstein, *Remarks on the Foundations of Mathematics*, ed. G. H. von Wright, Rush Rhees, and G. E. M. Anscombe, trans. G. E. M. Anscombe (Oxford: Basil Blackwell, 1978), 142e.

Despite the optimism of theorists such as Tegmark, the quagmire of non-Euclidean geometry, nonstandard algebra, paradoxes in set theory, and other disquieting mathematics have instilled a fear that mathematics is not discovering truths and may not have one universal foundation to support its work. This problem is noted by Hilbert: "In mathematics, this paragon of reliability and truth, the very notions and inferences, as everyone learns, teaches and uses them, lead to absurdities. And where else would reliability and truth be found if even mathematical thinking fails?"[56] It has been a long-held assumption that mathematics is our bastion of truth and reality. Consequently, the apparent problem of incompatible laws between, for instance, Euclidean and non-Euclidean geometries, led many to question "truth." Unfortunately, this is often a result of our typical notion of "truth," that is, to imagine that truth is something "out there" as an objective and external universal reality. Certainly, descriptive propositions about the world can be true or false, but Wittgenstein argues that the logical syntax of mathematics is often wrongly construed as true or false. In other words, mathematical syntax does not form a description of the world; it is not part of epistemology. Shanker correctly notes:

> For in all areas of the foundational spectrum mathematicians and philosophers were responding to the same species of worry. One might thus argue that the real culprit in the surge of foundationalism was the persistent intrusion of epistemology in those areas where it has no business to meddle. Epistemology has now extended its tentacles into virtually every aspect of philosophical thought, and for two millennia philosophers have stoutly battled with the spectre of the scepticism which it invariably bestows. Despite their preoccupation with the technical problems of analysis, not even pure mathematicians were immune from the doubts being voiced by the philosophers amongst them.[57]

[56] Shanker, *Wittgenstein and the Turning-Point*, 230.
[57] Ibid., 267.

An example of the confusion of conflating mathematics with epistemology can be seen in Euclid's understanding of a point to be that which has no parts, and if a point does not have an extension, then how many points are required to cover a space—an infinite number? Also, take the well-known Zeno's paradox of the tortoise racing the hare. If points are empirical, then the hare must get halfway from one point to the next, but to get there the hare must cross half the distance first, then the previous half, and so on ad infinitum. This problem is the consequence of treating mathematical propositions as empirical.

Another example of the problem of epistemology can be seen in the simple case of the aforementioned 2 + 2 = 4, and a "law of nature," such as Einstein's famous equation $E = mc^2$. Does the former contain apples or oranges, or the latter mass? Wittgenstein himself notes:

> I learned empirically that this came out this time, that it usually does come out; but does the proposition of mathematics say that? I learned empirically that this is the road I travelled. But is *that* the mathematical statement?—What does it say though? What relation has it to these empirical propositions? The mathematical proposition has the dignity of a rule. So much is true about saying that mathematics is logic: its movement is within the rules of our language. And this gives it its peculiar solidity, its unassailable position, set apart.[58]

Consequently, as Wittgenstein notes regarding language: "We cannot say of a grammatical rule that it conforms to or contradicts a fact. The rules of grammar are independent of the facts we describe in language … The words 'practical' and 'impractical' characterize rules. A rule is not true or false."[59] Likewise, the logical syntax of our mathematical propositions are not true or false as understood in traditional

---

[58] Wittgenstein, *Remarks on the Foundations of Mathematics*, Vol. 1, 164.
[59] Ludwig Wittgenstein, *Wittgenstein's Lectures, 1933–35: From the Notes of Alice Ambrose and Margaret Macdonald*, ed. Alice Ambrose (Chicago, IL: University of Chicago Press, 1989), 65, 70.

epistemology where empirical statements are contingently true or false until compared with the world.

What about a mathematical proof? We may assume there is a truth in the proof. However, consider the distinction between a mathematical proof and a proposition that "there are two computers in my office." The proof does not prove anything that exists prior to the proof. There were already two computers in my office before the proposition was formed and the subsequent empirical investigation. Yet in the case of the proof there is not something a priori behind the proof; instead, it is the proof itself that proves the rules of logical syntax in the proposition. The proof and the mathematical proposition are internal to each other—unlike the contingency of the proposition regarding how many computers are in my office.

Shanker rightly notes that "a mathematical proof is a grammatical construction, and thus a mathematical position is a grammatical convention, whose role is carved out by the internal relations established in the proof."[60] In other words, unlike empirical propositions, mathematical propositions as rules of syntax need to be grammatically understood—but this is not empirically verified. The propositions in language and mathematics are similar in that both must have an application—that is why they are both called propositions—but the proof and the mathematical proposition are internally related. Yet there is the constant search for an external and independent reality to justify our propositions. For example, Euclidean geometry was "demoted" since it no longer held an a priori status, and it was seen for what it is, namely, an autonomous axiomatic system that has its own rules of logic and uniformity. Yet why would this validate demotion? The reason is that it did not offer the "true" connection to reality. The problem realist mathematicians get into is that they focus on the entire realist system and Euclidean geometry no longer fits. What they miss is that Euclidean geometry is just one form of propositions within a system of propositions.

[60] Shanker, *Wittgenstein and the Turning-Point*, 53.

As Wittgenstein sees regarding language, there can be various language-games, and since there is no *one* language, it then follows that one does not supplant another. His philosophy of language, in terms of logic, then applies to the logic of math in a parallel manner. Both language and mathematics have propositions that are in a relation within their own system; however, since the nature of each is different, that is, the former are descriptions of the world while the latter are not, it follows that they are verified differently. The former are verified by checking the world while the latter are verified by means of their logical syntax. In other words, there is no isomorphism for language or mathematics—as if real numbers mirror those transcending us.

Although Wittgenstein notes that mathematical propositions are not to be justified epistemologically, he is not giving a metaphysical justification to the propositions. Instead, he shows that their logic is not based on an external independent foundation, but is internally related to the proposition itself. Winch rightly comments:

> Wittgenstein has many ways of characterizing grammatical propositions—"self-evident propositions", "concept-forming propositions", etc.—but one of the most important was in describing them as rules. In emphasizing the fluidity of the grammatical/material distinction, he was drawing attention to the fact that concept-formation—and thus the establishing of rules for what it does and does not make sense to say—is not something fixed by immutable laws of logical form (as he held in the *Tractatus*) but is something that is always linked with a custom, a practice.[61]

Wittgenstein abandons referential meaning, for example, that the meaning of a name is the object it links to, or a formal principle, and instead sees that a word only has meaning within a system of propositions and

---

[61] Ray Monk, *Ludwig Wittgenstein: The Duty of Genius* (London: Jonathan Cape, 1990), 468.

the rules within each system. Consequently, in terms of mathematics, Wittgenstein remarks:

> What does mathematics need a foundation for? It no more needs one, I believe, than propositions about physical objects—or about sense impressions, need an analysis. What mathematical propositions do stand in need of is clarification of their grammar, just as do those other propositions. The mathematical problems of what is called foundations are no more the foundation of mathematics for us than the painted rock is the support of a painted tower.[62]

It then follows that "it is essential to mathematics that its signs are also employed in civil life. It is the use outside mathematics, and so the meaning of the signs, that makes the sign-game into mathematics."[63] Moreover, "what we call 'counting' is an important part of our life's activities. Counting and calculating are not e.g. simply a pastime. Counting (and that means: counting like this) is a technique that is employed daily in the most various operations of our lives."[64] Hence, mathematics is not based on abstract forms, objects, formalism, logical atomism, or the like; rather, it takes form as applied within our form of life. Stenholm rightly says: "Mathematical texts are not descriptions of 'something'; they are the thing itself. Mathematics consists only in algebraic operations and derives no meaning from its outside. We cannot describe [explain] mathematics; we can only do it."[65] Likewise, Shanker notes that confusion is the result of "treating mathematical positions as a species of descriptive (empirical) proposition."[66]

Yet Wittgenstein sees the questions being asked:

> "But doesn't it follow with logical necessity that you get two when you add one to one, and three when you add one to two? And isn't

---

[62] Wittgenstein, *Remarks on the Foundations of Mathematics*, 171e.
[63] Ibid., Vol. IV, 2.
[64] Ibid., Vol. I, 4.
[65] Stenholm, *The Quest for Reality*, 173–4.
[66] Shanker, *Wittgenstein and the Turning-Point*, 31.

this inexorability the same as that of logical inference?"—Yes! It is the same.—"But isn't there a truth corresponding to logical inference? Isn't it true that this follows from that?"—The proposition: "It is true that that this follows from that" means simply: this follows from that.[67]

He uses the following analogy to show this point: "How should we get into conflict with truth, if our footrules were made of very soft rubber instead of wood and steel?—'Well, we shouldn't get to know the correct measurement of the table.'—You mean: we should not get, or could not be sure of getting, that measurement which we had with our ridged rulers."[68] The search for a justification for a mathematical proposition is a consequence of bringing in epistemology, while Wittgenstein sees that a mathematical proposition, unlike an empirical proposition that is contingently true or false as compared to the world, is not something we justify; rather, we have agreed that it is a rule.

What Wittgenstein does in language and mathematics is reject an external independent foundation of logic and metaphysical objects; of course, this leads many, given the prevalence of realism, to assume that he is providing a skeptical account of mathematics and turning it into a soup *de jour*. Tied to this is the thought that he must simply assume that mathematicians invent mathematics. The basic idea is that either mathematicians discover mathematical truths that were already "out there" waiting to be discovered or mathematicians "cook-up" mathematics, which in turn is fallible and open to revision and construction. Granted, Wittgenstein is commonly thought to lean toward the constructivist side, but it is entirely wrong to regard him as a constructivist. On the contrary, he rejects uncertainty and skepticism in mathematics, but not by offering further or better epistemological theories; instead, he drops epistemology and thereby also the foundational problems. It is important to realize that Wittgenstein is

---

[67] Wittgenstein, *Remarks on the Foundations of Mathematics*, 4e.
[68] Ibid.

not simply rejecting epistemology in toto; instead, he removes epistemology from, as it were, an illegitimate search for foundational theories for language and mathematics. In other words, he clarifies the role of epistemology.

What about subjectivism? As is the case regarding an invented language (private language), an invented mathematics would be, as Wittgenstein would say, nothing other than scribbles. Mathematical signs relate to our life through their grammatical rules, and it is these rules that make mathematics more than the formalists' scribbling games. Wittgenstein never denies objectivity; instead, he shows the nature of objectivity: it is in the form of life for language and the mathematical rules for mathematics, and while the former are descriptive the latter are not. So, the objectivity of mathematics does not rest on Platonic numbers or descriptions of reality; instead, it is internally related to the rules. Wittgenstein says: "What is interesting is how we use mathematical propositions. This is how calculation is done, in such circumstances a calculation is *treated* as absolutely reliable, as certainly correct."[69] Moreover, he notes that certainty is not a universal measure, but there is an empirical certainty and a mathematical certainty.[70] Again, Wittgenstein says that a mathematical proposition has "solidity" and an "unassailable position." Mathematical knowledge, once divested of epistemological considerations and an independent foundation, may seem to be heading away from certainty, but Wittgenstein wants to show the certainty mathematics does have, namely, its rules.

Yet how does this tie into science? Shanker rightly notes that when comparing mathematical and scientific propositions, we need not concern ourselves with epistemology and justifying the truth of the former, which would frequently lead us to "Platonist metaphysics— where meaningless pictures are called upon to do the work of philosophical clarification—or else into the realm of pseudo-scientific

---

[69] Wittgenstein, *On Certainty*, 38–9.
[70] Wittgenstein, *Philosophical Investigations*, §224.

jargon where the logico-grammatical barriers separating mathematics from science are consistently transgressed."[71] This confusion of confounding the epistemological with logical syntax and the empirical is difficult to dissect in physics in particular, where there must be an empirical verification. It becomes difficult to separate the empirical experiments with the mathematical constructions of reality. Indeed, as noted by Paul Davies: "Scientists often use the word 'discovery' to refer to some purely theoretical advance. Thus one often hears it said that Stephen Hawking 'discovered' that black holes are not black, but emit radiation. This statement refers solely to a mathematical investigation. Nobody has yet seen a black hole, much less detected any heat radiation from one."[72] Equally, but on a smaller scale, Davies also notes that

> quantum mechanics demolished the concept of an external state of reality in which all meaningful physical variables could be assigned well-defined values at all times [in contrast to the optimism of Galileo, Newton, and others]. So a subtle shift occurred ... in which the ground of reality first become transferred to the laws of physics themselves, and then to their mathematical surrogates, such as Lagrangians, Hilbert spaces, etc. The logical conclusion of going down this path is to treat the physical universe as if it is mathematics.[73]

However, as Bohr notes: "The difference between mathematics and the natural sciences proper rests on the fact that in the former, where we define the rules of the game ourselves, we can state the preconditions for definitions and concepts, whilst in the latter we must always be prepared to learn from new experiences that the usefulness of any form of description may be contingent upon previously unnoticed

---

[71] Shanker, *Wittgenstein and the Turning-Point*, 26.
[72] Paul Davies and John Gribbin, *Matter Myth: Dramatic Discoveries That Challenge Our Understanding of Physical Reality* (New York: Simon & Schuster Paperbacks, 2007), 18.
[73] Davies, *Information and the Nature of Reality*, 67.

preconditions."[74] The "surrogates" noted by Davies are reaching out with mathematical structures to create realms that they regard as reality, which clearly are not based on experience; but as Bohr noted, mathematics is based on rules and games that are not preconditions. In other words, the rule may depend on us, the ones who "define the rules of the game," but the truth of the rule does not depend on us—it, so to speak, depends on itself.

What does this mean for mathematics if we are defining its rules? As Wittgenstein says, "the mathematician is an inventor, not a discoverer."[75] Does this give freedom to invent mathematical realms? No, it does not. The development is not based on creating a larger or alternate universe or universes; rather, it is based on our experience. Wittgenstein compared language to an old city that develops and so does mathematics, as he says: "What, then—does it just twist and turn about within these rules?—It forms ever new rules: is always building new roads for traffic; by extending the network of old ones."[76] It is significant to note that the old roads, alternate axiomatic rules, are not simply rejected in favor of better roads, or even more drastically to assume that there are alternate cities for the new roads; rather, the old and new roads (i.e., the old and new rules) simply show the variety of rules we use. Likewise, Shanker notes:

> When a scientist chooses from amongst the alternative geometries which mathematicians have provided according to the nature of the phenomena which he is investigating, he is not ascertaining which geometry is the most "accurate" [universally] of the various contenders for the purposes which he has in mind. What he does discover, however, is simply the advanced utility of operating with a geometry in which it is intelligible to speak e.g. of a geodesic straight line. For the behaviour of a natural phenomenon is not part of the geometrical

[74] Niels Bohr, *Collected Works*, ed. David Favrholdt, *Complementarity beyond Physics (1928–1962)*, Vol. 10 (Netherlands: Elsevier Science, 1996), 504.
[75] Wittgenstein, *Remarks on the Foundations of Mathematics*, 47e.
[76] Ibid., Vol. I, 165.

concepts themselves; it is the framework against which these concepts are applied. If these framework conditions were to change, it would render these concepts not false, but most likely useless.[77]

Yet among physicists there are a few who nonetheless support the idea that since there are various outcomes in experiments and divergent possibilities, it is still useful to seek a determined and independent mathematical system. Consequently, in order to contain the many variants they create, for example, a multiverse. Shanker rightly notes that "the philosopher who resorts to possible world semantics has not strayed unawares into some unexpected domain; he has deliberately ventured into the void because like Jason he thinks he can return with the Golden Fleece, if only he has sufficient courage and perseverance."[78] Certainly, this is the case in the thought of Tegmark; his type of confusion is a consequence of forcing an ideal conception on reality. Regarding this type of confusion, Rhees notes: "We use mathematics in making measurements, and we commonly state our results as approximations to some mathematical proposition which is taken as the norm. If it brings any trouble, it is only when we try to give an account of what we are doing; if we imagine, for instance, that we hold up before our minds an ideal case and compare our products with that."[79] The "ideal case" is what the "mathematical surrogates" attempt to discover, that is, they try to imagine an ideal reality in contrast to the apparent rough ground we live on. Indeed, mathematicians can be caught in the idea that reality and truth are being discovered through mathematics and that this discovered reality is more wondrous than our own humble and rough roads. Yet, as Wittgenstein remarks:

> The only point there can be to elegance in mathematical proof is to reveal certain analogies in a particularly striking manner, when that is

---

[77] Shanker, *Wittgenstein and the Turning-Point*, 271.
[78] Ibid., 288.
[79] Rush Rhees, *In Dialogue with the Greeks, Volume I: The Presocratics and Reality*, ed. D. Z. Phillips (Burlington, VT: Ashgate, 2004), 95.

what is wanted; otherwise it is a product of stupidity and its only effect is to obscure what ought to be clear and manifest. The stupid pursuit of elegance is a principal cause of the mathematician's failure to understand their own operations; or perhaps the lack of understanding and the pursuit of elegance have a common origin.[80]

It is important here to note that Wittgenstein is not simply rejecting elegance; rather, he is saying that elegance in and of itself is not a mathematical pursuit. Like the Emperor focusing on the majesty of his new clothes while there is actually nothing there. Or as Søren Kierkegaard would say: "Like a man who builds an enormous castle and himself lives alongside it in a shed; they themselves do not live in the enormous systematic building."[81]

In contrast to the "mathematical surrogates," Bohr notes:

> It must be realized that the very definition of mathematical symbols and operations rests on a simple logical use of common language. Indeed, mathematics is not to be regarded as a special branch of knowledge based on the accumulation of experience, but rather as a refinement of general language, supplementing it with appropriate tools to represent relations for which ordinary verbal communication is imprecise or too cumbersome. Strictly speaking, the mathematical formalism of quantum mechanics and electrodynamics merely offers rules of calculation for the deduction of expectations about observations under well-defined experimental conditions specified by classical physics concepts.[82]

Likewise, Shanker says: "Mathematical propositions qua rules of syntax must (by definition) be grammatically—as opposed to epistemologically—intelligible."[83] Given this, it does not make sense

---

[80] Wittgenstein, *Philosophical Grammar*, 462.
[81] Søren Kierkegaard, *Soren Kierkegaard's Journals and Papers*, ed. and trans. Howard V. Hong and Edna H. Hong, assisted by Gregor Malantschuk, Vol. 3 (Bloomington and London: Indiana University Press, 1975), 519.
[82] Bohr, *Collected Works*, Vol. 10, 406.
[83] Shanker, *Wittgenstein and the Turning-Point*, 55.

to question whether or not mathematical propositions are inductive or not since they have a certainty based on their normative nature—and this makes doubts, as is the case in language as well, senseless. Again, as in the case of the old city it is significant that Bohr maintains classical physics as the expression of what we know within experience, just as the old roads are maintained. As Wittgenstein has shown, true and false are applied within the grammar of language and mathematics; they have no place empirically defining reality itself.

As will be discussed more fully later, the important point here is that what makes a physics proposition true is that it meets with observation; however, what it meets with is not simply observation, it is what we observe in the particular experimental arrangements. The language regarding the observation follows a particular grammar and mathematical syntax that are part of our form of life. In other words, the logic shown in the language of physics is internal to that very language, and this logic is neither true nor false; however, what is said after an experiment is itself true or false based on what is observed and mediated by language.

Wittgenstein rejects the idea that numbers inhabit an external reality (realism) and he also rejects the idea that numbers are nothing more than marks on paper (formalism); instead, through use and application numbers become mathematics. Likewise, rather than a name standing in for a simple object, as was the case in the *Tractatus* (logical atomism), he later showed that words in a language hold meaning within a system of propositions, and logic is not underlying this system as a guarantor of uniformity and meaning; instead, logic is found in the propositional system. In other words, what is key here is not an independent external reality, but the logical syntax of what we say and how we do mathematics—their use. It is a Platonist confusion to think that all the points together of a curve means the curve exists; instead, Wittgenstein would say the curve is the rule. When mathematicians think that an expansion is surveyable they fall to

Wittgenstein's criticism, namely: "There is no religious denomination in which the misuse of metaphysical expressions has been responsible for so much sin as it has in mathematics."[84]

As noted previously, Wittgenstein does indeed turn from epistemology to logic. In the *Tractatus* he says: "Logic must take care of itself"[85] and in *On Certainty* he notes: "Logic cannot be described." "You must look at the practice of language, then you will see it."[86] Wittgenstein's point in his later work is still logic, but he turns away from epistemology to the logic found in our propositions and rules—not the logic under our propositions and rules.

---

[84] Wittgenstein, *Culture and Value*, 1.
[85] Wittgenstein, *Tractatus Logico-Philosophicus*, 5.473.
[86] Wittgenstein, *On Certainty*, 501.

3

Physics and the Fly-Bottle

The problem referred to earlier, of the separation between the mind, or if preferred sense-experiences, and an external reality, can also be seen as the problem between materialism and idealism. For instance, materialism is the thought that there is a physical world that provides sense-experiences to gain the required data for knowledge, whereas idealism regards one's mind as the source of knowledge. Thus, it is interesting that Heisenberg notes: "It is remarkable that this old question of materialism and idealism has again been raised in a very definite form by modern atomic physics and particularly by the quantum theory."[1] As shown earlier, Wittgenstein would regard this question in the following manner: "One man is a convinced realist, another is a convinced idealist and teaches his children accordingly. In such an important matter as the existence or non-existence of the external world they don't want to teach their children anything wrong."[2]

To engage this discussion I focus primarily on quantum theory and, in particular, on how Bohr's thought and what has become known as the Copenhagen interpretation add further insights in line with the earlier Wittgensteinian discussion. Just as Wittgenstein saw that it is a confusion to separate language and numbers from our form of life, and thereby posit a foundation that is an external independent and a priori reality, the same is true within Bohr's physics—both were upset when positivists accepted and defended their work. At the same time, neither are idealists.

---

[1] Heisenberg, *On Modern Physics*, 6.
[2] Ludwig Wittgenstein, *Zettel*, ed. G. E. M. Anscombe and G. H. von Wright, trans. G. E. M. Anscombe (Oxford: Basil Blackwell, 1967), §413.

Bohr's work, and the Copenhagen interpretation more generally, have provided quantum investigations that have changed our perception of reality from a clockwork system to a much more dynamic and unpredictable reality. Henry Stapp notes that the Copenhagen interpretation, "eschewed ontology."[3] Indeed, John Wheeler realized that the laws of physics came into being "higgledy-piggledy ... There was no tablet of granite with the laws chiseled on it in advance!"[4] The belief that the universe is self-generating is not a result or consequence of science; instead, it is a worldview that overlays one's science (materialism). Moreover, laws do not create or explain, for example, gravity; rather, they are descriptive.[5] The laws of nature are instrumental to physics, but they cannot hold some a priori status to which nature therefore complies. As Nancy Cartwright rightly notes: "What modern science seems to show is not that we live in a world governed by a single systematic set of natural laws that apply at all times and in all places, but rather that we live in a 'dappled world' in which pockets of order emerge, or can be made to emerge, using a patchwork of different scientific theories ... none of which is applicable across all domains."[6] Moreover, Polkinghorne says: "What had been considered to be an arena of clear and determinate process [i.e., Newtonian physics] was found to be, at its subatomic roots, cloudy and fitful in its behavior."[7] Clearly, the resemblance to Wittgenstein cannot be missed, that is, his understanding of language changed from it being based on a uniform independent logical syntax to the rough ground and intertwined among various roads. Equally, Bohr says: "Our washing up is just like our language ... we have dirty water and dirty dishcloths, and

---

[3] Henry Stapp, "Minds and Values in the Quantum Universe," in *Information and the Nature of Reality: From Physics to Metaphysics*, ed. Paul Davies and Niels Henrik Gregersen (Cambridge: Cambridge University Press, 2010), 112.
[4] John Wheeler, "The Computer and the Universe," *International Journal of Theoretical Physics*, 21, nos. 6–7 (1982), 565.
[5] Lennox, *God and Stephen Hawking*, 40–1.
[6] See Dixon, *Science and Religion*, 48.
[7] Polkinghorne, *Quantum Theory*, preface.

yet we manage to get the plates and glasses clean."[8] Wittgenstein, in line with the move away from reductionism, pointed out that there is not one strand, but a network of strands from which we understand reality.

In contrast to determined systems based on a discovery of an external and independent reality, Heisenberg says: "What is really needed is a change in the fundamental concepts. We will have to abandon the philosophy of Democritus and the concept of fundamental elementary particles."[9] It is telling that Heisenberg also says: "I am convinced that this intense search for quarks is caused by the conscious or unconscious hope of finding the really elementary particles, the ultimate units of matter."[10] Just as language does not mirror reality, or simple objects, why should we expect physical reality to mirror the quantum world? More specifically, Anton Zeilinger comments: "A criticism of realism also emerges from the notion of complementarity. It is not just that we are unable to measure two complementary quantities of a particle, such as its position and momentum, at the same time. Rather, the assumption that a particle possesses both position and momentum before the measurement is made is wrong."[11]

Given that reality was beginning to lose its mechanical cog and wheel functions, there was a shift to focusing on theory, that is, theories about a nature that is apparently disjointed—but should not be. These theories are based on mathematical formulations and formed a mathematical reality, in contrast to a reductionist account of physical reality. A possible resultant confusion is to place an empirical syntax into quantum theory even though the quantum "world"

---

[8] Heisenberg, *Physics and Beyond*, 137.
[9] Heisenberg, *Tradition in Science*, 17. It is telling that Heisenberg also says: "I am convinced that this intense search for quarks is caused by the conscious or unconscious hope of finding the really elementary particles, the ultimate units of matter. But even if quarks could be found, from all what we know they would again be divided into two quarks and one antiquark etc.; they would not be more elementary than a proton." Ibid., 16–17.
[10] Heisenberg, *Tradition in Science*, 16–17.
[11] Anton Zeilinger, "The Message of the Quantum," *Nature*, 438, no. 7069 (2005), 743.

is a mathematical model. Classical physics refers to objects, but as Heisenberg says: "Planck's action quantum … does not represent a property of objects, but a property of nature."[12] Honner thereby rightly notes: "Bohr does not offer a precise account of knowledge and understanding. He does not attempt to describe the structure of knowing or to establish a foundational epistemology."[13] Even more strongly, Heisenberg says that "Bohr would not like to say that nature imitates a mathematical scheme."[14] Realism leads physicists, as is the case in mathematics, to often confuse empirical propositions with mathematical propositions and models, rather than staying with the logic of the latter.

Rhees notes that it is problematic to use "ordinary language to describe what we expressed in mathematical terms when we were measuring—using our instruments and calculating to see how near we had brought it [an ideal case]—we should never have imagined that we were comparing our job with an ideal case (which we could not imagine, and which would be of no help anyway)."[15] Likewise, Wittgenstein rejects ostensive definition, since names are not always in a name-object relation. Indeed, often names do not necessarily name something, contrary to Wittgenstein's early thinking where the simple objects were the base of language. For example, Wittgenstein notes that for "ow!"[16] even though there is no determined simple object, in fact there is nothing a priori existing for the word "ow," there is an application. The same is true in line with Bohr's thought, namely, we get into confusion when we turn to determined preexisting particles that we are naming; instead, we need to see their meaning in application. According to Honner, Bohr "does not choose to

---

[12] Heisenberg, *On Modern Physics*, 7.
[13] Honner, *Description of Nature*, 147.
[14] Werner Heisenberg, Interviewed by T. S. Kuhn, February 25 and 27, 1963, Archive for the History of Quantum Physics, transcripts, 26.
[15] Rhees, *In Dialogue with the* Greeks, Vol. 1, 95.
[16] Wittgenstein, *Philosophical Investigations*, §27.

begin with a foundational epistemology resting on an absolute and permanent bedrock of privileged word-world relationships."[17] Thus, for Bohr "there is a fluidity between our words and our world: each discloses the other just as much as it warrants the other."[18] Science builds on evidence, but it is a mistake to assume that mathematical models are directly tied to concrete and determined objects. Certainly, once a measurement is made, such as the position of a particle, then a particle has a position and this is empirical, but the quantum theory and rules are not, in and of themselves, empirical. As Wheeler notes, "no elementary phenomenon is a phenomenon until it is a registered (observed) phenomenon."[19]

Despite Bohr's rejection of a classically determined reality, he still used classical physics to describe observations. He says: "Only with the help of classical ideas is it possible to ascribe an unambiguous meaning to the results of observation."[20] This is Bohr's correspondence between the classical and the quantum dynamics. It was initially seen as problematic (and still is by many); however, he later saw that it was the way to understand the quantum realm. As Honner says: "One can ... observe an evolution in his thought: in his writings the emphasis shifts from 'classical concepts' to 'concepts of our ordinary, everyday world'; and such a shift runs directly parallel to the revision of the Correspondence Principle itself."[21] Indeed, Honner says that "in notes from 1957 Bohr crossed out the words 'classically defined' and replaced them with 'communicable in ordinary language.' "[22] In a sense, Bohr uses correspondence less and less, perhaps similar to how Wittgenstein moved away from the idea of language corresponding with an underlying logic, that is, there is no strict underlying determinist micro world

---

[17] Honner, *Description of Nature*, 73.
[18] Ibid., 159.
[19] Wheeler, *The Computer and the Universe*, 560.
[20] Bohr, *Atomic Theory and the Description of Nature*, 17.
[21] Honner, *Description of Nature*, 62.
[22] Ibid.

in either case; we communicate and have meaning in the, so to speak, classical macro world. Léon Rosenfield says that Bohr's concern was that "the use of words in everyday life must then be subject to the condition that they be kept within the same plan of objectivity; and as soon as we deal with words referring to our own thinking, we are exposed to the danger of gliding onto another plane."[23] This is like Wittgenstein and ordinary language: the only way to have meaning is in contrast to language "idling"; and logic is in the ordinary language we use, just as the quantum is in the measuring. Bohr thereby turns "arguments based on thought-experiments into arguments about observation and language."[24] For example, when Wittgenstein read Heinrich Hertz he was taken with how

> Hertz addresses the problem of how to understand the mysterious concept of "force" as it is used in Newtonian physics. Hertz proposes that, instead of giving a direct answer to the question: "What is force?", the problem should be dealt with by restating Newtonian physics without using "force" as a basic concept. "When these painful contradictions are removed", he writes, "the question as to the nature of force will not have been answered, but our minds, no longer vexed, will cease to ask illegitimate questions."[25]

Bohr's "logical demand" is that "it is a necessary condition for the possibility of unambiguous communication that suitably refined everyday concepts be used, no matter how far the processes concerned transcend the range of ordinary experience."[26] Moreover, according to Honner, Bohr would hold that "we can know an external reality, but the knowing is more by participation than by some sort of abstraction at a distance."[27]

---

[23] Léon Rosenfield, "Niels Bohr's Contribution in Epistemology," *Physics Today*, 16 (1963), 49, 54.
[24] Honner, *Description of Nature*, 119.
[25] Monk, *Duty of Genius*, 26.
[26] Honner, *Description of Nature*, 88.
[27] Ibid., 68.

This is comparable to Wittgenstein's private language and the language-game. Phillips notes that formerly Wittgenstein thought that "the determination of sense makes it necessary to arrive at some kind of criterion for what *can* and *cannot* be said. By the time Wittgenstein wrote the *Investigations*, he had moved away from this position. Instead of claiming that logic determines what *can* and *cannot* be said, he asks us to look at the logic, or the grammar, as he puts it, of what is said."[28] Likewise, Bohr notes: "It is wrong to think that the task of physics is to find out how Nature is. Physics concerns what we can say about Nature."[29] Additionally, Zeilinger says that "the most fundamental viewpoint here is that the quantum is a consequence of what can be said about the world."[30] Just as Wittgenstein always looked for the particular, hence the various language-games, Bohr saw that "the possibility of a comprehensive picture should perhaps not be sought in the generality of the point of view, but rather in the strictest possible limitation of the applicability of the points of view."[31] As Honner says, for Bohr "there is no universal and independent scientific language; rather, we can only use descriptive concepts objectively when we include an account of the context in which they are applied."[32]

What we do say uses classical terminology, but how is it used? When using classical physics terminology to describe experimental results regarding the quantum, it shows the above-mentioned "fitful" world of quantum dynamics. This points to the logic of Bohr's understanding, which is most well known as complementarity. Wheeler notes: "Bohr's principle of complementarity is the most revolutionary scientific concept of this century and the heart of his fifty-year

---

[28] Rush Rhees, *Wittgenstein and the Possibility of Discourse*, ed. D. Z. Phillips (Cambridge, England: Cambridge University Press, 1998), 3.
[29] A. Petersen, "The Philosophy of Niels Bohr," in *Neils Bohr: A Centenary Volume*, ed. A. P. French and P. I. Kennedy (Cambridge: Harvard University Press, 1985), 299.
[30] Zeilinger, "A Foundational Principle for Quantum Mechanics," 642.
[31] See Honner, *Description of Nature*, 76.
[32] Ibid., 153.

search for the full significance of the quantum idea."[33] The correspondence principle (between the classical terminology and the experimental quantum measurements) lead to complementarity and the Copenhagen interpretation. In other words, the only way to have any understanding of the quantum, and the only thing we can say, is what is discovered through experiment in terms of classical language. Bohr says that the quantum "forces us to replace the ideal of causality by a more general viewpoint usually called complementarity."[34] As Heisenberg remarks: "The laws of nature formulated in mathematical terms no longer determine the phenomenon themselves, but the possibility of happening, the probability that something will happen."[35] Quantum mechanics does not describe a determined and discrete reality; rather, it predicts possible realities; as Bohr notes: "Quantum mechanics and quantum electrodynamics make use of a formalism which does not allow interpretation by means of accustomed physical pictures and aim only at deriving probabilities for the occurrence of individual events observable under well-defined experimental conditions."[36] Wittgenstein would by analogy agree that there is no essence or ostensive definition of meaning; it is through use (measuring) that we come to know.

Heisenberg's uncertainty principle, not knowing a particle's position and momentum in any exact measurement simultaneously,[37] and the perplexing wave and particle nature, were noted by Bohr in terms of complementarity, that is, there is no contradiction in these apparently contradictory ideas; rather, they complement each other. As Polkinghorne says: "An electron does not all the time possess a definite position or a definite momentum, but rather it possesses the

[33] John Wheeler, "No Fugitive and Cloistered Virtue—a Tribute to Niels Bohr," *Physics Today*, 16 (Jan. 1963), 30.
[34] Niels Bohr, "Causality and Complementarity," *Philosophy of Science*, 4, no. 3 (1937), 291.
[35] Heisenberg, *On Modern Physics*, 10.
[36] Bohr, *Collected Works*, Vol. 10, 178–9.
[37] It is important to note that it is not the case that the particle has a position, and that we simply do not know it until it is measured; rather, there is no position until measurement.

potentiality for exhibiting one or other of these if a measurement turns the potentiality into an actuality."[38] Additionally, Erwin Schrödinger notes: "Everything—*really everything*—is simultaneously particle and field. Everything has the continuous structure that is familiar to us from the field, as well as the discrete structure familiar to us from the particle. ... The difficulty, which is equal in all cases, of combining these two widely different characteristics in one mental picture is still today the major obstacle that makes our image of matters so variable and uncertain."[39] The reason for the apparent contradiction, according to Bohr, was the experimental condition that was mutually exclusive; for example, you cannot measure both the wave and particle nature simultaneously. To get a measurement for the position of a single particle requires one to measure position, and this yields discrete information, while to learn of the motion of the quantum yields continuous and regular information (wave equation). There is no singular entity in existence—until it is measured.[40]

This should sound similar to Wittgenstein's insistence that words have meaning necessarily tied to their use in our language, and logic is shown in the resultant language, that is, words and logic are emergent. Likewise, Paul Davies says that "decoherence and wave packet collapse are well explained by appealing to quantum interactions with the wider environment. ... There is no longer any need to invoke mysterious extra ingredients, or rules that emerge at the 'measurement level,' even though the 'collapse of the wave packet' is legitimately an emergent phenomenon."[41] Many imagined that local realism was a given, that particles have particular properties independent of measurement. Therefore, given the lack of a clear and deterministic realm,

---

[38] Polkinghorne, *Quantum Theory*, 86.
[39] In Heisenberg, *On Modern Physics*, 42–3.
[40] It is interesting to add that the desire of classical theism to maintain Divine simplicity compares to the physicist's desire to have a uniform theory to avoid human participation and change.
[41] Paul Davies and Philip Clayton, *The Re-emergence of Emergence: The Emergentist Hypothesis from Science to Religion* (Oxford: Oxford University Press, 2006), 37.

some physicists thereby posit hidden-variable theories to explain things we do not know yet, but with more understanding of physical reality they assume that one day we will be able to keep realism alive.

It is apparently extraordinarily difficult for many to accept the lack of an external and independent reality that simply waits to be discovered by a detached observer. Zeilinger notes Pauli writing:

> To me it seems quite adequate to call the conceptual description of nature in classical physics, which Einstein wants to keep so emphatically, the ideal of the detached observer. In drastic words the spectator must, according to this ideal, appear in a fully discrete manner as a hidden spectator. He can never appear as an actor. Nature is hereby left alone in its predetermined course of events, without regard to the manner in which the phenomena are observed.[42]

For example, Einstein writes in a reply to one of Bohr's letters:

> Quantum mechanics is very impressive. But an inner voice tells me that it is not yet the real thing. ... It is only in the quantum theory that Newton's differential method becomes inadequate, and indeed strict causality fails us. But the last word has not yet been said. May the spirit of Newton's differential method give us the power to restore unison between physical reality and the profoundest characteristic of Newton's teaching—strict causality.[43]

Einstein's thought is comparable to Wittgenstein's in the *Tractatus*, where language was thought to mirror the underlying independent logical syntax, but clearly diverges from Wittgenstein's later thought, where language emerges through our use and practices. Rhees notes, regarding Wittgenstein:

> Much of the discussion of the uniformity of nature seems to be of how we are justified in looking for a cause or a law. This question does

---

[42] Anton Zeilinger, "Vastakohtien todellisuus," in *Festschrift for K. V. Laurik Ainen*, ed. U. Ketvel et al. (Helsinki: Helsinki University Press, 1996), 174.

[43] In Abraham Pais, *Subtle Is the Lord: The Science and the Life of Albert Einstein* (Oxford: Oxford University Press, 2005), 443.

not normally arise in science. And in any case, it does not affect the question of the validity—i.e. the conclusiveness—of any conclusion that is derived from experiment or observation. The suggestion is that unless you are justified in looking for a cause, or for any general law, then no conclusion will have any "probability". But this is meaningless. It is almost like asking whether we can (n. b.) trust science. Perhaps amounting to asking whether perhaps the results of science are just a fluke.[44]

Traditionally, and perhaps continually, science does not question whether or not one should look for the cause or law, and certainly there is the thought that such categories inform us, but why? One answer is the desire to ground causality.

According to Bohr: "The causal mode of description has deep roots in our conscious endeavors to utilize experience for practical adjustment to our environments, and is in this way inherently incorporated in common language. By the guidance which analysis in terms of cause and effect has offered in many fields of human knowledge, the principle of causality has even come to stand as the ideal for scientific explanation."[45] Once causality and continuity are questioned, as is the case in quantum theory, then the classically disposed physicists are left hanging. Moreover, as Bohr notes:

> A wholly new situation in physical science was created through the discovery of the universal quantum of action, which revealed an elementary feature of "individuality" of atomic processes far beyond the old doctrine of the limited divisibility of matter originally introduced as a foundation for a causal explanation of the specific properties of material substances. This novel feature is not only entirely foreign to the classical theories of mechanics and electromagnetism, but is even irreconcilable with the very idea of causality.[46]

---

[44] Wittgenstein, "Wittgenstein's Philosophical Conversations with Rush Rhees," 46.
[45] Bohr, "On the Notions of Causality and Complementarity," 51.
[46] Ibid.

The ideal cause and effect relation is determinism, in which case instantaneous momentum and position are known; indeed, known through all time. However, this is not the case with the quantum. In other words, our classical conception is naive. It is not as deterministic as thought. There is a clear drive to find causality at the bottom or in a hidden quality—something to connect apparent "individual" quantum events and thereby get rid of complementarity. However, the problem is not the micro, it is our conception of the macro.

Bohr brings his quantum realization to the macro and it fits in with Wittgenstein's philosophy. The problem is not the separation between the quantum and the classical, or the micro and the macro, and then to see how to tie them together; they were never separate in the first place. The former is internal to the latter—there is no transition or barrier. An important point is that it makes no sense to question how our macro world is built on the micro world; rather, we know that the micro is set by the macro (our observation/measurement/system). In other words, the micro is internal to the macro as the rule is internal to the logical syntax.

Bohr's complementarity is analogical to Wittgenstein's understanding of language, that is, the circular aspect of our use and the independent aspect of it. Language does not independently create reality, just as experiments and the observer do not independently create reality. Instead, reality is, so to speak, in language and the experiments of observers. This is neither realism nor nonrealism. There is not one language that we can reduce or explain; language, like reality, cannot be bound or entirely determined. In short, language is composed of language-games, which are systems composed of propositions. Likewise, Bohr says: "Evidence obtained under different experimental conditions cannot be comprehended within a single picture, but must be regarded as *complementary* in the sense that only the totality of the phenomena exhausts the possible information about the objects."[47] So, just as there are language-games, all of which are autonomous yet together make language, so our interaction with autonomous experiments at the quanta level taken together is reality. The mistake is to assume that one language-game, or one experiment, is a building block of data working out and leading to the one determined cause-effect reality set on an a priori foundation. The logical baggage of realism haunts current discussions of quantum and religion. Indeed, Honner notes: "If Bohr's approach is not recognized as more circular (that is, as acknowledging the hermeneutic circle of language and reality) than axiomatic or architectonic, then it will remain baffling."[48]

It is interesting to note that Giambattista Vico (1668–1744) had already noticed the importance of complementarity in philosophy, as Emanuel Paparella states: "As an antidote to rampant Cartesian rationalism, Vico, way back in 1725 ... perceived that the whole of reality operates on two paradoxically related and complementary poles ... for example ... objective/subjective. This complementarity issues forth not from rationalistic pseudo-unity of intellectual categories but rather from an organic unity derived from the phenomena of its very origins."[49] Hence the importance of classical descriptions and Wittgenstein's ordinary language are in use, while also seeing the distinct nature of reality and logic within these. However, complementarity challenges our common understanding of logic with notions of a "hermeneutic circle" and "paradoxically related and complementary poles."

For instance, quantum logic clearly does not rest well with traditional logic—Aristotelian logic—since it is not simply true or false when dealing with the quantum. Polkinghorne notes that classical

---

[47] Honner, *Description of Nature*, 90.
[48] Ibid., 73.
[49] Emanuel L. Paparella, *Hermeneutics in the Philosophy of Giambattista Vico: Vico's Paradox; Revolutionary Humanistic Vision for the New Age* (San Francisco: EMText, 2003), 47.

logic (such as Aristotle's) does not apply to quantum logic: "An electron can not only be 'here' and 'not here', but also in any number of other states that are superpositions of 'here' and 'not here'. That constitutes a middle term undreamed of by Aristotle."[50] This is the superposition principle. In his article titled "An experimental test of non-local realism," Zeilinger and colleagues point out that our usual conceptions of "Aristotelian logic, counterfactual definiteness, absence of actions into the past or a world that is not completely deterministic are questionable given the experimental observations."[51]

This should point out that the quantum realm (excluding a particular measurement) is not true or false, but, as Wittgenstein has noted, neither are the rules of mathematics; and these models of mathematics form our quantum understanding. The problem here is the theory of the seemingly disjointed nature of the quantum, but this can be dissolved once we see the different logic at work. This is not a problem of ontology or epistemology. In other words, it is not a matter of our own lack of knowledge, which some day will understand the cause-effect and determinism of the quantum realm. Logic is not a universal norm known as Aristotelian logic. It is true that classical terminology and Aristotelian logic are used to understand the quantum, yet we need to see that the quantum itself is not grounded in classical terms and Aristotelian logic. In other words, classical terms and Aristotelian logic show us what the quantum is like. If, however, we use the term "proposition," then we need to see that it is used in a new way. Wittgenstein notes:

> The word "proposition", if it is to have any meaning at all here, is equivalent to a calculus: to a calculus in which p v − p is a tautology (in which the "law of the excluded middle" holds). When it is supposed not to hold, we have altered the concept of proposition. But that does

---

[50] Polkinghorne, *Quantum Theory*, 37–8.
[51] Simon Gröblacher et al., "An Experimental Test of Non-local Realism," *Nature*, 446, no. 7138 (2007), 871–5 (quote 875).

not mean we have made a discovery (found something that is a proposition and yet doesn't obey such and such a law); it means we have made a new stipulation, or set up a new game.[52]

This new game is the logic of the quantum. Can we say that it is the logical syntax of the wave function that is in superposition? So the problem is not the transition from micro to macro, but to see the distinction between the logical syntax of quantum rules contra quantum observations and measurements. The wave function is not external to the rule; it is the rule. Confusion arises when the wave function is conflated as an empirical object.

Similar to Wittgenstein and the language-game, where a word is only understood within a game, Bohr notes: "In the case of quantum phenomena, the unlimited divisibility of events implied in such an account is, in principle, excluded by the requirement to specify the experimental conditions. Indeed, the feature of wholeness typical of proper quantum phenomena finds its logical expression in the circumstance that any attempt at a well-defined subdivision would demand a change in the experimental arrangement incompatible with the definition of the phenomena under investigation."[53] The point here is that the contradictory nature of the quanta is a consequence of applying Aristotelian logic and realism to the quantum. While quantum logic is different, as Wittgenstein notes regarding language and mathematics, grammar is not true or false and mathematical rules are not true or false. Is the rule comparable to the quantum and the extension to the particle? Not quite, since the particle is external (empirical) and the extension is not (it is internal to the rule). This is why Wittgenstein's point is important: "How a proposition is verified is what it says. Compare generality in arithmetic with generality of non-arithmetical

---

[52] Wittgenstein, *Philosophical Grammar*, 368.
[53] Niels Bohr, "Quantum Physics and Philosophy," *Essays 1958–1962 on Atomic Physics and Human Knowledge*, The Philosophical Writings of Niels Bohr, Vol. III (Woodbridge, CT: Ox Bow Press, 1987), 4.

propositions. It is differently verified and is of a different kind. The verification is not a mere token of truth, but determines the sense of the proposition. (Einstein: how a magnitude is measured is what it is.)"[54] In effect, there are two logics, one causality and the other complementarity. Wave-particle duality is not a contradiction, but is a contrariety, and therefore can be a "fruitful source of empirical application as in Euclidean and non-Euclidean geometry."[55] Perhaps one way to see this is that the wave-particle duality is simply the logical rule and, again, remember that the logical rules are not true or false, rather they work or they do not; therefore, it is not a logical either-or contradiction to have a complementarity. However, this view would be unbearable for a realist or logical atomist bent on proving the uniformity of the independent reality "out there" to which we connect, even though Bohr says we "are not dealing with more or less vague analogies, but with clear examples of logical relations which, in different contexts, are met with in wider fields."[56] Moreover, he notes: "In quantum mechanics, we are not dealing with an arbitrary renunciation of a more detailed analysis of the atomic phenomena, but with a recognition that such an analysis is *in principle* excluded."[57]

Consequently, Bohr sees that a new conception is required:

> The old question of an ultimate determinacy of natural phenomena has lost its conceptual basis, and it is against this background that the viewpoint of complementarity presents itself as a rational generalization of the very ideal of causality. The complementary mode of description does indeed not involve any arbitrary renunciation of customary demands of explanation but, on the contrary, aims at an appropriate dialectic expression for the actual conditions of analysis and synthesis in atomic physics. Incidentally, it would seem that the recourse to three valued logic, sometimes proposed as means for dealing with the

---

[54] Wittgenstein, *Philosophical Grammar*, 458–9.
[55] Shanker, *Wittgenstein and the Turning-Point*, 253.
[56] Bohr, *Essays 1958–1962 on Atomic Physics and Human Knowledge*, Vol. III, 7.
[57] Bohr, *Essays 1932–1957 on Atomic Physics and Human Knowledge*, Vol. II, 62.

paradoxical features of quantum theory, is not suited to give a clearer account of the situation, since all well-defined experimental evidence, even if it cannot be analyzed in terms of classical physics, must be expressed in ordinary language making use of common logic.[58]

The answer is that the quantum world is composed of mathematical formations that are themselves neither true or false nor in-between, the "maybe" that displaces the Aristotelian excluded middle. A. A. Grib writes: "In the quantum logical interpretation, truth values for properties must be given by a Boolean observer. Without the observer 'true' is only a nondistributive 'structure' of the lattice. ... Non-Boolean, nondistributive logic is nonhuman logic; the observer must 'translate' nonhuman quantum logic into his Boolean language. This 'nonhumaness' of quantum logic is the expression of the 'objectivity' of quantum objects."[59] The problem is conflating the wave function with an empirical reality, but it is a tool/technique, just as pure mathematics is a technique—not a proposition. We cannot use propositions in a classical sense to determine discrete properties of particles before measurement. The difference in logic is that empirical propositions have evidence (checked with how the world is), while mathematical propositions do not have evidence; instead, they are verified grammatically (construction of rules of logical syntax).

There is no meaning without interaction; this applies to words/language and physical objects. As Simon Kochen writes: "Quantum mechanical properties are not intrinsic to the system, but have truth values created by interactions with other systems."[60] Wittgenstein notes that mathematics, such as geometry, and like language, functions by means of a syntax that shows the logical rules for that particular application in a system, that is, the grammar of describing the

---

[58] Bohr, "On the Notions of Causality and Complementarity," 54.
[59] A. A. Grib, "Quantum Logical Interpretation of Quantum Mechanics: The Role of Time," *International Journal of Theoretical Physics*, 32, no. 12 (1993), 2395.
[60] Simon Kochen, "A Reconstruction of Quantum Mechanics," *Foundational Physics*, 45, no. 5 (2015), 562.

phenomena.⁶¹ Likewise, for the quantum, there is an application to a system, yet it is a system that shows a nature that is at odds with typical classical systems. Bohr says: "The mutually exclusive relationship which will always exist between the practical use of any word and any attempts at its strict definition."⁶² This is because there is no definition, as Wittgenstein would say, outside practical use. He notes: "All testing, all confirmation and disconfirmation of a hypothesis takes place already within a system. And this system is not a more or less arbitrary and doubtful point of departure for all our arguments; no, it belongs to the essence of what we call an argument. The system is not so much the point of departure, as the element in which arguments have their life."⁶³

Despite the complex discussions regarding the quantum, it is certainly the case that the calculations work. Polkinghorne notes that "quantum electrodynamics ... yields results that agree with experiment to an accuracy corresponding to an error of less than the width of a human hair in relation to the distance between Los Angeles and New York!"⁶⁴ The problem does not reside in the calculations; rather, it is the theories. This fits with Wittgenstein, where meaning is in use, our form of life, not in theory or explanation. He says: "Am I not getting closer and closer to saying that in the end logic cannot be described? You must look at the practice of language, then you will see it."⁶⁵ The point is that rather than thinking of a logical syntax underlying language and determining what can and cannot be said, he instead looks at what we do say—that our measurements work. What we do say does not depend on explanatory justifications; instead, it is directly tied to our use of language and our form of life, and it is

---

[61] Ludwig Wittgenstein, *Ludwig Wittgenstein and the Vienna Circle: Conversations Recorded by Friedrich Waismann*, ed. B. F. McGuiness and J. Schulte, trans. B. F. McGuinness (Oxford: Basil Blackwell, 1979), 38, 162f.
[62] Bohr, *Essays 1932–1957 on Atomic Physics and Human Knowledge*, Vol. II, 52.
[63] Wittgenstein, *On Certainty*, 105.
[64] Polkinghorne, *Quantum Theory*, 40.
[65] Wittgenstein, *On Certainty*, 51.

through these that logic is shown. In this case the uniformity that is the continual quest of the realists is not an underlying structure, but is our form of life.

The exit

Realism is so ingrained in our thought that we typically have an incredibly difficult time conceiving any other way of understanding reality—except perhaps nonrealism. However, as noted above, nonrealism is simply the flip side of realism, as Berkeley is the flip side of empiricism. In the case of quantum physics, it is equally difficult to get out from under the weight of realism in terms of determinism, causality, and foundationalism. Once again, Polkinghorne notes that although the calculations can be practiced, there is no theory that explains why this is the case; indeed, working through interpretive problems "will demand for their eventual settlement not only physical insight but also metaphysical decision."[66] Polkinghorne is right, except that what is required is a clarification of our understanding of reality that does not rest on the metaphysical. Even Heisenberg, given the clear problems of a reductionist and foundational physical system, had difficulty conceiving of a way to deal with the reality he found; hence, he considers returning to Plato.[67] But Wittgenstein says: "A metaphysical question is always in appearance a factual one, although the problem is a conceptual one."[68] This is exactly what happens when the logic of the empirical is placed in the quantum realm. Metaphysical explanations are not the goal, nor are mathematical formulations; again, as Zeilinger notes regarding a foundational type principle: "I do not mean an axiomatic formalization of

---

[66] Polkinghorne, *Quantum Theory*, preface.
[67] Heisenberg, *Tradition in Science*, 17.
[68] Ludwig Wittgenstein, *Remarks on the Philosophy of Psychology*, Vol. 1, trans. G. E. M. Anscombe (Oxford: Basil Blackwell, 1980), §949.

the mathematical foundations of quantum mechanics, but a foundational conceptual principle."[69] A different conception, a different way of looking, is what is required.

Rhees writes in a letter to M. O'C. Drury:

> Wittgenstein was trying to combat the view that all investigation "tries to become" causal investigation or is a fumbling attempt in that direction. / "Providing a different way of looking at it"—this is constantly the work of philosophy. For this reason we may speak of philosophy as contemplative. And this is nothing like the work of science. / "No, it does not have to be like this. But this is how it is." / Considering different possibilities may help you to see how it is; whereas the search for explanations and causes may keep you from looking.[70]

The difficulty is not only escaping the fly-bottle, but more significantly, seeing the problem of the fly-bottle in the first place. Wittgenstein remarks:

> What makes a subject hard to understand—if it's something significant and important—is not that before you can understand it you need to be specially trained in abstruse matters, but the contrast between understanding the subject and what most people want to see. Because of this the very things what are most obvious may become the hardest of all to understand. What has to be overcome is a difficulty having to do with the will, rather than with the intellect.[71]

The reason there is so much "resistance of will" is because we wrongly assume that that which we are explaining resides in some foundation beyond us, be it God or the foundation of the physical world, namely, particles. We need to see that we and our surroundings are the foundations, and we describe these, we do not explain them; just as we do not explain our consciousness; rather, we are conscious. The various

---

[69] Zeilinger, "A Foundational Principle for Quantum Mechanics," 631.
[70] Wittgenstein, "Wittgenstein's Philosophical Conversations with Rush Rhees," 39n. 103.
[71] Wittgenstein, *Culture and Value*, 17e.

theories explain and posit an external foundation abstracted from our human reality.

Rather than seeking hidden variables to resolve the current difficulties regarding the foundation of reality, what happens if we instead reconsider our conception and participation in reality? Could reality be participation between the physical and life? Could it be the case that the observer, in a sense, forces space-time onto the quanta? These questions are not directed to epistemology, but to the logic shown in what we know and say. However, once in the fly-bottle it is difficult to see the need to backtrack rather than continue going forward against its sides. For example, Einstein notes:

> I cannot substantiate my attitude to physics in a way that you would find rational. I see, of course, that the statistical interpretation ... has a considerable content of truth. Yet I cannot seriously believe it, because the theory is inconsistent with the principle that physics has to represent a reality in space and time, without the ghost of action at a distance ... I am absolutely convinced that we shall eventually arrive at a theory in which the objects connected by laws are not probabilities, but facts, such as one took for granted only a short time ago. However, I cannot provide logical arguments for my conviction. I can only call on my little finger as a witness, which claims no authority outside my own skin.[72]

Einstein was convinced that the answer could be found in the fly-bottle, yet it is interesting that he nonetheless says that he "cannot provide logical arguments" for his point. Alternatively, it is interesting to note Rosenfield's remark:

> [In 1961] I had occasion to discuss Bohr's ideas with the great Japanese physicist [Hideki Yukawa], whose conception of the meson with its complementary aspects of elementary particle and field of nuclear force is one of the most striking illustrations of the

---

[72] Max Born, *Natural Philosophy of Cause and Chance* (Oxford: Clarendon Press, 1949), 122.

fruitfulness of the new way of looking at things that we owe to Neils Bohr. I asked Yukawa whether the Japanese physicists had the same difficulty as their Western colleagues in assimilating the idea of complementarity ... He answered "No, Bohr's argumentation has always appeared quite evident to us; ... you see, we in Japan have not been corrupted by Aristotle."[73]

The calculations work for Einstein and for Yukawa, but their respective conceptions are entirely different. According to Honner: "Einstein is not so much mistaken about his criterion of reality as about his understanding of the valid application of concepts."[74]

This is difficult territory to enter, that is, speaking of our conceptual understanding and stepping out of traditional classical physics and realism (including nonrealism) discussions. Yet it is necessary to do so. Could physics itself provide the answer? I do not think so; physics cannot explain the concepts we have about physics. As Honner says: "Even in classical physics, however, the concepts employed to describe any system are created by the subject. One does not discover concepts in nature."[75] And as Davies says: "The laws of physics are inherent in and emergent with the universe, not transcendent of it."[76] This understanding of concepts regarding the universe fits Wittgenstein's remark on concepts:

> If the formation of concepts can be explained by facts of nature, should we not be interested, not in grammar, but rather in that nature which is the basis of grammar?—Our interest certainly includes the correspondence between concepts and very general facts of nature. (Such facts as mostly do not strike us because of their generality.) But our interest does not fall back upon these possible causes of the formation of concepts; we are not doing natural science; nor yet natural

---

[73] Léon Rosenfeld, "Niels Bohr's Contribution to Epistemology," *Physics Today*, 16 (Oct. 1963), 47.
[74] Honner, *Description of Nature*, 140.
[75] Ibid., 145.
[76] Davies, *Information and the Nature of Reality*, 83.

history—since we can invent fictitious natural history for our purposes. I am not saying: if such-and-such facts of nature were different, people would have different concepts (in the sense of a hypothesis). But: if anyone believes that certain concepts are absolutely the correct ones, and that having different ones would mean not realizing something we realize—then let him imagine certain very general facts of nature to be different from what we are used to, and the formation of concepts different from the usual ones will become intelligible to him.[77]

Of course, the implication is not that concepts "float" outside nature. The point is that we do not find concepts lurking about independent of us. Even Einstein had a glimpse of this, as Heisenberg notes: "It is generally believed that our science is empirical, and that we draw our concepts and our mathematical constructs from empirical data. … [and he recalls Einstein saying] 'This may have been my philosophy, but it is nonsense all the same. It is never possible to introduce only observable quantities in a theory. It is the theory which decides what can be observed.'"[78]

Rather than understanding a foundation as the smallest irreducible (or the most eloquent mathematical formula), we need to see that the search for a foundation does not make sense. What does make sense is to realize that what we call reality is our form of life. Phillips notes that Rhees "wants to deny that language has the unity of a calculus, or the unity of a game. He wants to say that the unity language has is the unity of a common intelligibility."[79] Indeed, as Polkinghorne says: "It is *intelligibility* (rather than objectivity) that is the clue to reality."[80] We can work through a mathematical notation, but it is only through dialogue that it can make sense since it is not just formal connections

---

[77] Wittgenstein, *Philosophical Investigations*, part two, xii.
[78] Heisenberg, *Tradition in Science*, 10.
[79] Rhees, *Wittgenstein and the Possibility of Discourse*, 12.
[80] Polkinghorne, *Quantum Theory*, 86.

that lead to intelligibility. In other words, dialogue and intelligibility are not grounded on a formal structure. Language is not a type of calculation that one learns to extend; rather, it is variable and intelligibility is key, that is, one's form of life. As Honner notes: "Despite the certitude which mathematical treatments lent to physics, conceptual accounts were still dependent for their meaning on the circumstances of the subjects who use them."[81]

I suggest that the word "true" is misunderstood; for example, when we say 2 + 2 = 4 is true, this is actually not true or false; it is the given of mathematical rules. It is only true if we take two pens and add another two to our basket and say: "Two pens plus two pens, that's four pens." Interestingly, Richard Feynman recounts his early days of learning mathematics: "Understanding the whole idea was to find out what x is—it doesn't make any difference how you do it ... Doing it 'by algebra' was a set of rules which, if you followed them blindly, could produce the answer ... a series of steps by which you could get the answer if you didn't understand what you were trying to do. The rules had been invented."[82] Likewise, one can make a mistake in a calculation, yet how is a mistake understood regarding one's opinion in life? When we have an understanding of something, it is not simply more knowledge of a formal system or logical analysis; instead, there is an increase in intelligibility that clearly moves through time. In other words, our conception of time is directly tied to further intelligibility, which in itself is through the unity of language. Would a determinate causal process preclude our conception of time and a growth in intelligibility?

Wittgenstein is not interested in what can be said (as the limit), but what we do say (as the limit). Importantly, as should be clear, the latter can change! Phillips notes: "What is ruled out is not ruled out by logic,

---

[81] Honner, *Description of Nature*, 144.
[82] Richard Feynman, *What Do You Care What Other People Think? Further Adventures of a Curious Character* (New York: W. W. Norton, 1988), 17.

but by the language-game; or, if you like, by the logic of the language-game."[83] This is often missed. Just as Zeilinger correctly remarks: "The stochasticity of the individual event in the quantum measurement process" is largely unappreciated; "the question arises which features such a philosophical foundation might have."[84] One application is to Wittgenstein, who says: "Then is there something arbitrary about this system? Yes and no. It is akin to both what is arbitrary and to what is non-arbitrary."[85] In other words, there is no underlying determinate reality that already is set and therefore determines what we can say and measure; rather, what we say and measure *is* the determination. Without randomness and indeterminacy, there is determinism and causality. If there were only determinism and causality, then we could not consider the *possibility* of determinism and causality.

Wittgenstein's interest in logic is not like the logic in Russell's *Principia Mathematica*; rather than logical principles he is interested in how logic is shown in language; it is the given, and describing this is the logic. For example, Wittgenstein says: "If I believe that I am sitting in my room when I am not, then I shall not be said to have *made a mistake*. But what is the essential difference between this case and a mistake?"[86] The logic here is that a mistake does not belong to this particular language-game and is thereby logically ruled out. It is this logic that Wittgenstein is interested in, and it points to our conceptions (language).

Discussions of our conceptual understanding, in contrast to mathematical axioms and empirical data, can easily fall into wild speculation and various sorts of mysticism; as is very clear, given the abundance of peculiar discussions and books that connect quantum theory to almost anything. Moreover, as noted earlier, there is even a general impression that Bohr became less rigorous in his thinking

[83] Phillips, *Wittgenstein's on Certainty*, 141.
[84] Zeilinger, "Interpretation and Foundation of Quantum Mechanics," 167.
[85] Wittgenstein, *Zettel*, 358.
[86] Wittgenstein, *On Certainty*, 195.

in his later years. Certainly Bohr rejected crass materialism, but he also rejected wild mysticism.[87] It is simply the case, as Bohr rightly notes, and along Wittgensteinan lines, that "in any communication of experience, we have to rely on some conceptual frame which is common for those between [whom] the communication takes part, but that we must be prepared—as we see in science and in all regions of life that new experience can demand in order to remove inconsistencies or disharmonies—to take recourse to a wider frame. That's just a general lesson of mathematics."[88] It is clear that concepts are important, but the problem is that they are often and wrongly separated from reality.

The first step to clarify our conception of reality is, once again, to see the problematic and ingrained Cartesian separation of the subject from the object, that is, the individual from the external world. For Bohr, the nature of the quantum is similar to the nature of debates in philosophy over object and subject.[89] As Honner notes: "Einstein separated concept and sense-experience, so that science was seen to offer an account of the world's comprehensibility which mirrored reality."[90] Zeilinger also comments on this problem: "The Cartesian divide—the separation between *res cogitans* (that which thinks) and *res extensa* (that which is out there)—had deeply penetrated the human soul during the three centuries after Descartes. For Heisenberg, this was why the epistemological paradigm on which one could build the foundations of quantum mechanics had not been found yet."[91] Moreover, as Richard Bernstein notes: "We need to exorcise the Cartesian anxiety and liberate ourselves from its seductive appeal."[92] It is interesting that those who critique any discussion of the role of the observer—and

[87] Honner, *Description of Nature*, 148.
[88] Bohr, *Collected Works*, Vol. 10, 189.
[89] Honner, *Description of Nature*, 78.
[90] Ibid., 113.
[91] Anton Zeilinger, "The Quantum Centennial," *Nature*, 408 (Dec. 2000), 641.
[92] Richard Bernstein, *Beyond Objectivism and Relativism: Science, Hermeneutics, and Praxis* (Philadelphia: University of Pennsylvania Press, 1983), 9.

reject it as, for example, subjectivism—miss that what we call reality, in part, creates the observer.

Clearly, neither Wittgenstein nor Bohr reject objectivity. For example, Bohr remarks:

> It is essential to remember that all unambiguous information concerning atomic objects is derived from the permanent marks ... left on the bodies which define the experimental conditions ... The description of atomic phenomena has in these respects a perfectly objective character, in the sense that no explicit reference is made to any individual observer ... As regards all such points, the observation problem of quantum physics in no way differs from the classical physical approach.[93]

Yet he and Wittgenstein do reject a misleading conception of objectivity, namely, one that assumes a complete separation from human life and from concepts. Heisenberg notes: "As Karl von Weizsäcker has said, 'Nature existed before man'. That is to say, nature certainly existed before man existed, but if nature existed before man, it is not the same as the natural sciences. For example, the concept of 'the law of nature' cannot be completely objective, the word 'law' being a purely human principle."[94] Note that denying the active role of the observer/participant is, in a sense, the more subjective position since it focuses on the self as independent from nature/reality (or, of course, is identical with nature and therefore the question is moot, as nonrealism is the flip side of realism). It is a two-way path: if we influence nature, we must realize that nature influences us.

Similar to Wittgenstein, Wheeler says: "Useful as it is under everyday circumstances to say that the world exists 'out there' independent of us, that view can no longer be upheld. There is a strange sense in which this is a 'participatory universe.'"[95] Likewise, as Honner

---

[93] Honner, *Description of Nature*, 66.
[94] Heisenberg, *On Modern Physics*, 26.
[95] Wheeler, "The Computer and the Universe," 564.

notes: "Bohr's notion of objectivity differs from the classical account ... in that he stresses that our descriptions of nature are not descriptions of independently existing realities, but descriptions of *our encounters with* such realities."[96] Bohr himself says: "We are both onlookers and actors in the great drama of existence: this is the old truth of which the new situation in physics ... has so forcibly reminded us."[97] And Zeilinger writes:

> In physics we cannot talk about reality independent of what can be said about reality. Likewise it does not make sense to reduce the task of physics to just making subjective statements, because any statements about the physical world must ultimately be subject to experiment. Therefore, while in a classical worldview, reality is a primary concept prior to and independent of observation with all its properties, in the emerging view of quantum mechanics the notions of reality and of information are on an equal footing. One implies the other and neither one is sufficient to obtain a complete understanding of the world.[98]

It is clear that there is some participatory relation between us and the universe.

Heisenberg sees that the problem of working out the relation between the objective and the subjective can fall into two main groups: one being the "essence of matter" and the other an "epistemological problem, which particularly since Kant has been repeatedly raised, of how far it is possible to objectify our observations of nature—or our sensory experience in general—that is, to determine from observed phenomenon an objective process independent of the observer."[99] Kant is an interesting figure since he is regarded as a forerunner of changing our conception of the relation between our

---

[96] Honner, *Description of Nature*, 146.
[97] Bohr, *Atomic Theory and Description of Nature*, 119.
[98] Zeilinger, "A Foundational Principle for Quantum Mechanics," 642.
[99] Heisenberg, *On Modern Physics*, 4.

minds and the world. He says that "the mere ... consciousness of my own existence proves the existence of objects in space outside me."[100] He then also notes the significance of the interplay between our concepts and reality: "Thus far it has been assumed that all our cognition must conform to objects. On that presupposition, however, all our attempts to establish something about them a priori, by means of concepts through which our cognition would be expanded, have come to nothing. Let us, therefore, try to find out by experiment whether we shall not make better progress in the problems of metaphysics if we assume that objects must conform to our cognition."[101] He understood that we cannot, through reason alone, deal in metaphysical "truths." Instead, we necessarily gain knowledge from our interaction with the physical world; however, we are not simply passive recipients of knowledge from an external world—we are active in this knowledge. According to Kant, our part to play in gaining knowledge comes from a priori (before experience of the world) concepts, such as space and time. In other words, space and time for Kant are placed within our minds and we then organize our perceptions of the phenomenal world accordingly. That is, the physical world conforms to our internal category of space-time.

Wheeler raises a significant question: "How interesting it would be if one armed with modern insights would undertake afresh the program of Kant's *Kritik*. Would he find that the very conditions for apprehending sense data force space-time upon us, not the separate space and time that Kant thought he had derived?"[102] Kant rightly distinguished, as Wittgenstein also did, the empirical, and forms and categories, in opposition to realism and idealism. Fergus Kerr notes that "Wittgenstein was influenced by reading Ludwig Boltzmann (1844–1906), the Austrian physicist with whom he considered studying ...

---

[100] Immanuel Kant, *Critique of Pure Reason*, trans. Werner S. Pluhar, introduction by Patricia W. Kitcher (Indiananpolis: Hackett, 1996), 289.
[101] Ibid., 21.
[102] Wheeler, "The Computer and the Universe," 559.

Boltzmann's ideas were to be strongly attacked by the logical positivists, as it happens; but his distinctly Kantian view of science, in which our models of reality are taken to our experience of the world, and not the other way round, no doubt inoculated Wittgenstein for good against anything like the so-called British empiricist tradition."[103] Wittgenstein dissolves the bits of realism in Kant's thought by showing that there cannot be a conception of space-time separated from our experience of objects; instead, space-time is shown in our language. With Kant, Wittgenstein saw that our concepts cannot be based on a simple reduction to physical objects and sense perceptions, but he differs by not basing such a thing in our minds, but in language. Unlike Kant, for whom transcendental idealism makes our minds a foundation, Wittgenstein instead shows that our form of thought is not in our mind but in language. Moreover, time is a consequence of change, and our form of life, so time is not an a priori category in our minds. Consider space-time in a black hole and at the quantum level—the stopping of time. In contrast to Kant spacetime is a concept forced on us by language (in our form of life). That reality is based on a shared language, and that this forms our concepts that are in flux, shows us space-time: none of this is based on causality. In other words, language is in space-time, and time is the growth of understanding that is a consequence of change, which itself is not based on causality.

Kant's *noumenal* is an external category, whereas Wittgenstein shows that reality is internal to language, and that reality is our form of life. In other words, information is directly tied to the physical world, and we could not even have thoughts without it (space-time). Likewise, Bohr uses the term "phenomena" simply to mean the observation given the experimental arrangement; he was not speaking of

---

[103] Fergus Kerr, *Work on Oneself: Wittgenstein's Philosophical Psychology*, Institute for the Psychological Sciences Monograph Series, Vol. 1 (Arlington, VA: Institute for the Psychological Sciences Press, 2008), 4.

a Kantian thing in itself distinct from our perception of it; rather, as Carl Friedrich von Weizsäcker notes: "If one wants to talk of such 'things', then they were ... to be found *in* the phenomena rather than behind it."[104] Additionally, Wittgenstein notes: "If you demand a rule from which it follows that there can't have been a miscalculation here, the answer is that we did not learn this through a rule, but by learning to calculate."[105]

Wittgenstein's thought also allows for contingencies rather than Kant's absolute and transcendental categories, such as mathematics and logic. Wittgenstein says: "The insidious thing about the causal point of view is that it leads us to say: 'Of course, it had to happen like that,' whereas we ought to think: it may have happened *like that*—and also in many other ways."[106] A system of probability is not the consequence of hidden variables or one's lack of knowledge; it is the system. Rhees notes: "There is something strange in the notion of an ideal of intelligibility which is not intelligible. Perhaps it is just a way of saying, 'Don't ever try to say: These are the principles of logic.'"[107] Or as Feynman said, regarding Descartes's idea that our imperfect thoughts show the necessity of the perfect: "Not at all! ... In science you can talk about relative degrees of approximation without having a perfect theory. ... I think it's a bunch of baloney."[108] What becomes prominent, in contrast to basic sense-experience or an a priori concept is, as Wheeler says: "Physics gives rise to observer-participancy; observer-participancy gives rise to information; and information gives rise to physics."[109] Or, as Zeilinger puts it: "The distinction between reality and our knowledge of reality, between reality and information, cannot

---

[104] In Honner, *Description of Nature*, 68.
[105] Wittgenstein, *On Certainty*, 44.
[106] Wittgenstein, *Culture and Value*, 37.
[107] Rhees, *In Dialogue with the Greeks*, Vol. 1, 109.
[108] Feynman, *What Do You Care What Other People Think?*, 29.
[109] John Wheeler, "Information, Physics, Quantum: The Search for Links," Proceedings of the 3rd International Symposium on Foundations of Quantum Mechanics (Tokyo, 1989), 313–14.

be made. There is no way to refer to reality without using the information we have about it."[110] Moreover, as Israel Belfer notes, Jacob Bekenstein "characterized what happened as the reversal of the horse and carriage.... Information theory was the horse, completely subordinate to the physical modeling process that was its driver."[111] Put in the strongest terms, Wheeler says: "I am in the grip of a new vision, that *Everything Is Information*. The more I have pondered the mystery of the quantum and our strange ability to comprehend this world in which we live, the more I see possible fundamental roles for logic and information as the bedrock of physical theory."[112]

Rather than getting caught in the realists' fly-bottle, and consequently bouncing back and forth between realism and idealism, or even Kant's insight that still is addressing and caught in the problem, we need to leave realism. Not only in philosophy, but also in physics. How? The way of language in philosophy, as understood by Wittgenstein, is also the way in physics as tied to information. Ultimately, language removes the foundation of our minds and sense-experience, and the foundation of metaphysical categories. Yet, as Honner rightly notes, we often have a problematic conception even of language: "In the classical view, moreover, in which the concepts and formulae of physical theory are taken to correspond to and represent real independent objects, there is an underlying assumption of a universal scientific language which is subject-independent."[113] Not only are concepts frequently separated from reality, but we are also even more likely to wrongly view language as a connection to an external reality—as our sense-experience connects to an external reality. Certainly there is some sense to this, but it can potentially

---

[110] Zeilinger, "The Message of the Quantum," 743.
[111] Israel Belfer, "Jacob Bekenstein and the Informational Turn in Theoretical Physics," *Physics in Perspective*, 16 (2014), 75.
[112] John Archibald Wheeler, *Geons, Black Holes and Quantum Foam: A Life in Physics* (New York: W. W. Norton, 1999), 64.
[113] Honner, *Description of Nature*, 153.

misconstrue our conception of reality (as already noted, regarding sense-experience). This was the problem with Locke: he placed the knowledge of physical objects external to us, by means of the sense data, in us; while Berkeley collapsed the problem of the separation between internal knowledge and external physical objects and ended up replacing physical objects with an exclusive "in our mind" knowledge. Of course, someone could reject Berkeley's God and posit a materialism whereby our minds are nothing other than an extension of physical forces.[114] In any case, what we need to see, in contrast to such theories, is that our knowledge of physical objects is directly tied to our conception of physical objects, and it is our language that is the nexus of this knowledge. Rhees notes: "To study language apart from the sort of importance it has in the circumstances in which it is learned, the sort of importance it has in living, is to take a false view of it. (The same is true of mathematics. This is what is wrong about speaking of mathematics as a game.)"[115] Likewise, Honner says: "In the final analysis, objectivity lay in the refinement of unambiguous communication based on well-defined use of pictures and ideas referring to events of daily life."[116] It is important to note, in contrast to linguistic idealism, that language and reality are in a complementary relationship; as Dilman notes: "While Wittgenstein rejects a language-independent reality he is clear that there is a two-way dependence between our language and the reality that constitutes the surroundings of our life, and indeed a two-way interaction between them."[117] Correspondingly, Honner says Bohr "does not begin with an 'inner-outer' distinction and then try to justify the independent existence of that which is 'without'. Instead, he first of all presumes the existence of

---

[114] This opens a new discussion of "mind"; however, I will only point out that it is peculiar that the physical world could in any way be thought of as independent from a language that is to describe it since such independence and description would be excluded. Or, put another way, how does a physical—exclusively physical—reality reflect on itself?

[115] In Wittgenstein, "Wittgenstein's Philosophical Conversations with Rush Rhees," 17–18.

[116] Honner, *Description of Nature*, 146.

[117] Dilman, *Wittgenstein's Copernican Revolution*, 170.

a reality of which we are a part, and then seeks to establish valid ways of communicating about that reality."[118]

I use the term "language matrix" to describe our understanding of, and participation with, reality. It is the matrix, as it were, of information and reality. This, in a sense, takes the foundational weight off our minds (subjectivity) and the physical world (objectivity). This fits with Bohr's remark: "Physics is to be regarded not so much as the study of something *a prior* given, but rather as the development of methods for ordering and surveying human experience. In this respect our task must be to account for such experience in a manner independent of individual subjective judgment and therefore objective in the sense that it can be unambiguously communicated in common human language."[119] Furthermore, Heisenberg notes:

> When we speak about our investigations, about the phenomena we are going to study, we need a language, we need words, and the words are the verbal expression of concepts. In the beginning of our investigations, there can be no avoiding the fact, that the words are connected with the old concepts, since the new ones don't yet exist. Therefore these so-called prejudices are a necessary part of our language, and cannot simply be eliminated. We learn language by tradition, the traditional concepts form our way of thinking about the problems and determine our questions.[120]

Likewise, Dilman notes that, for Wittgenstein, language is like "an ancient city to which new suburbs can be added—new language-games can develop. But before this happens language is not incomplete. The forms of reality that come into being did not exist unknown to us before the new language-games came into being."[121] In other words, there is no language or physical world that people created ex

---

[118] Honner, *Description of Nature*, 140.
[119] Bohr, *Essays 1958–1962 on Atomic Physics and Human Knowledge*, Vol. III, 10.
[120] Heisenberg, *Tradition in Science*, 15.
[121] Dilman, *Wittgenstein's Copernican Revolution*, 138.

nihilo; rather, these things form us. At the same time, our reality is not a reality that is entirely external to us since it is our language and participation that form our conception of that reality.

Zeilinger describes his understanding of language as follows: "Our physical description of the world is represented by propositions. Any physical object can be described by a set of true propositions. A complete description of an object in general is a very long list of propositions."[122] He is right in principle, but he is leaning very close to the typical idea that language is based on sense perceptions, and then placing the sense perceptions as primary in a causal relation with the object. The given is thought to be the structure between a proposition and the world, that there is a logical connection between the world as it is and the proposition; this is what propositions then have in common and guarantees meaning. Our sense-data or experimental data link to what is the given, and this is taken by many as the norm. Bertrand Russell maintained a causal relation between physical reality and our words, whereby the latter and their meaning must through a causal logical relationship connect with the objects they refer to. Wittgenstein was also initially interested in elementary propositions and a causal relation between a name and the simple object; however, he later questions the idea that a name or the data we have can be self-referential, that is, how can meaning reside in a sign itself? Just as it is wrong to take a word as a sign of an object, it is wrong to think of a particle as a determined part of a quantum realm.

Wittgenstein later emphasized the meaning of a proposition—which is its use. The object cannot be separated from language, logic is not an a priori independent category that language mirrors, and there is no reduction to simple objects as a foundation for meaning. There is not a causal or logical connection to an object that provides intelligibility. Instead, the meaning of the proposition and its logic are shown through our application of language. That is, we

[122] Zeilinger, "A Foundational Principle for Quantum Mechanics," 633.

learn about the physical world and logic in language, just as we learn mathematics by calculating. We only understand the "elementary system" if there is a composite system first, that is, language; and in the case of physics, the classical world of physics. Zeilinger is right when he says: "It is the simple fact that an elementary system cannot carry enough information to provide definite answers to all questions that could be asked experimentally,"[123] which clearly is the case for Wittgenstein's early Tractarian name-object relation, which is, as it were, a grammatical vacuum.

The quantum realm, like language, is in a state of possibilities, and only on a measure and within a proposition in an application is there a particular meaning for a particle or word. Wittgenstein rejects the Tractarian picture theory and instead turns to the language-games. Formerly he said: "We can say straight away: Instead of: this proposition has such and such a sense: this proposition represents such and such a situation. It portrays it logically. Only in this way can *the proposition* be true or false: It can only agree or disagree with reality by being *a picture* of the thing named."[124] And: "The great problem round which everything I write turns is: Is there an order in the world *a priori*, and if so what does it consist in?"[125] Like classical physics, Wittgenstein formally thought there was an a priori reality that we represent through pictures/propositions and it does not depend on our experience. However, Wittgenstein turns from his *Tractatus* view, which gave "logical space" (the space of possible facts) a platonic category, to removing the realism from this logical space and placing language-games as primary and as necessarily tied to human use. Likewise, the physicist does not simply have a pure sense-experience as a consequence of an experiment; rather, they observe the results mediated through language, and the grammar of language is not founded on any experiment or empirical observation.

[123] Ibid., 636.
[124] Wittgenstein, *Notebooks*, 8.
[125] Ibid., 53.

We need to reconsider not only our concepts and language, but also logic and the empirical. Dilman says that "our language is not founded on an empirical reality with which we are in contact through sense perception. Rather our language determines the kind of contact we have with such a reality and our conception of it."[126] Like the measuring instrument, language describes things external, but reality (e.g., our conceptions, type of investigation) is internal to both. However, the true or false potential of what either refers to does not depend on either when describing or measuring a state in our world. For example, there is no position, momentum, or, in a sense, even a particle until it is measured, only a set of probabilities. Bohr writes: "In contrast to ordinary mechanics, the new mechanics does not deal with a space-time description of the motion of atomic particles."[127] What this shows is not that language or the instrument creates reality, but that the interaction between the physical world and the instrument shows a measurement of reality. The actual numerical number regarding a particle position, for instance, does not depend on the observer; however, the meaning of the measurement is internal to our language—our concepts.

There is an intimate connection between language and physical reality, just as there is between intelligibility and physical reality. Neither singularly creates the other. Moreover, neither is determined by a causal relation, but are potentialities. Wittgenstein notes: "The rules of grammar are arbitrary in the same sense as the choice of a unit of measurement. But that means no more than that the choice is independent of the length of the objects to be measured and that the choice of one unit is not 'true' and another 'false' in a way that a statement of length is true or false."[128] The unity we observe in our world (language and physical) is a consequence of agreement through our language and measuring activities. This agreement does not decide

---

[126] Dilman, *Wittgenstein's Copernican Revolution*, 76.
[127] Bohr, *Atomic Theory and the Description of Nature*, Vol. I, 48.
[128] Wittgenstein, *Philosophical Grammar*, 185.

what is true or false; it is an agreement that allows us to see what is true or false.

Wittgenstein says: "Could one say that arithmetical or geometrical problems can always look, or can falsely be conceived, as if they referred to objects in space whereas they refer to space itself?"[129] Moreover,

> the stream of life, or the stream of the world, flows on and our propositions are so to speak verified at instants. Our propositions are only verified by the present. And so in some way they must be commensurable with the present; and they cannot be so in spite of their spatio-temporal nature; on the contrary this must be related to their commensurability as the corporeality of a ruler is to its being extended—which is what enables it to measure.[130]

This is similar to the stream of life as the statistical probabilities being formed in the present and verified when measured, and this gives them their spatial-temporal nature, that is, propositions and particles have a similar nature. We can only understand what is tied to a measure (rule), not despite the spatio-temporal, but because of it. This is *not* a reductionism. On the other hand, for Hugh Everett, mathematical entities of a theory are real. The problem here is that proponents of the multiverse conflate a mathematical equation with an actual empirical reality. This is the problem that Bohr was trying to avoid, and Wittgenstein also rejects this since he focuses on the logical syntax of mathematics and rejects the epistemological and ontological realms, and this would include a rejection of the many possible worlds. While Wittgenstein set a limit to facts and simple objects in the *Tractatus* to ensure uniformity, the many-world theory does the opposite: it includes all facts!

For classical physics and Everett's many-world idea, there is actually no information since there is nothing new, it is deterministic, so

---

[129] Ibid., 365.
[130] Wittgenstein, *Philosophical Remarks*, 81.

we at best discover causal relations. In contrast, and in line with the Copenhagen interpretation, Wittgenstein says: "You must bear in mind that the language-game is so to say something unpredictable. I mean: it is not based on grounds. It is not reasonable (or unreasonable). It is there—like our life."[131] With this viewpoint emergence is possible, that is, new facts, and this is then information that is not simply discovered—it is formed. The point is that any systematic structure for language, as it can or cannot connect to reality, misleads us from the actual application of language. This points to the lack of any necessity and determinism in what we do say. That is, there is no external connection, but there are connections within our use of language. This internal connection is what provides an expansion of understanding since it is not just a matter of "all the better" following the logical principles and rules. This internal connection means more than following a particular technique or rules. Instead, freedom is involved. Likewise, in the physical world, a freedom is seen in the quanta—which deny a complete description. Our judgments in our language and conceptions, and the quanta in the physical realm, provide freedom.

Rather than seeking a traditional foundation for our language and information, we need to see that these, as the language matrix, exist in, and are conditioned by, our world of possibilities. The nature of possibilities is not such that there are determinate possibilities, of which one is realized. Rather, within possibilities we have language and meaning formed. The language matrix in and of itself is possibilities, that is why the language-game is unpredictable; however, once there is a tradition and use of a particular language-game then the possibility has been set. This is like the quantum, where particles are unpredictable, but once measured, there is a set nature of the particle. Language is not fixed on an a priori pattern, it is a potentiality like the quanta. As Honner says: "It is the continuity of macroscopic objects

---

[131] Wittgenstein, *On Certainty*, §559.

in space and time which makes language stable, he [Bohr] might argue, and which gives basic descriptive concepts their univocity."[132] Boltzmann already saw that statistical laws apply to large populations of molecules, in contrast to observations regarding a molecule itself, and the Euclidean versus non-Euclidean depends on the particular system being discussed.

In contrast to extending the empirical, Dilman remarks: "But at the limits of what can be ascertained, verified and justified empirically, lies grammar, or what belongs to grammar, and that cannot be justified empirically."[133] There is a difference between logic and the empirical. We can empirically check if my dog is in the backyard or has escaped, where a particle hits a plate, but if we consider physical reality itself, there is no empirical point; rather, it is a logical point, that is, the logic of the reality of physical objects and of our grammar (the realm of possibilities that is neither true nor false)—both of which include the independent existence of physical objects. Yet, and importantly, that very logic is not independent of language. In other words, whether we are discussing empirical propositions or not, all our propositions have a similar context, that is, the language matrix in our form of life.

Dilman's remark has an interesting similarity to the quantum:

> What a grammatical remark articulates is the *form* of the language we use in saying something, not its *content*, i.e. what we say. The latter may be true or false, and is in any case independent of what we claim; but the form of grammar is what makes it possible for us to claim what we do claim, be it true or false. It is the form of the instrument of language which enables us to make the kind of claim we make.[134]

---

[132] Honner, *Description of Nature*, 85.
[133] Dilman, *Wittgenstein's Copernican Revolution*, 76.
[134] İlham Dilman, *Philosophy as Criticism: Essays on Dennett, Searle, Foot, Davidson, Nozick*, ed. Brian Davies and Mario von der Ruhr (New York: Continuum, 2011), 34.

This shows a comparison, namely, grammar with statistical probabilities, the form with the wave function, and the content, what we say, with the observation (particle). This is the distinction between the mathematical principles (logic) and the empirical. This is the language matrix that shows our understanding of reality through language, and sets the stage for a clearer discussion between science and religion outside the fly-bottle. The language matrix shows the logic of language and the quantum. One that shows a unity while also allowing possibilities. This is not a realist account since it does not separate logic or language or our concepts from an independent physical reality. Yet the logic, the grammar, and the probabilities are not empirical—rather they allow us to say what we do regarding the empirical.

4

Religion and the Fly-Bottle

Ray Monk notes Wittgenstein saying:

"Russell and the parsons between them have done infinite harm, infinite harm." Why pair Russell and the parsons in one condemnation? Because both have encouraged the idea that philosophical justification for religious beliefs is necessary for those beliefs to be given any credence. Both the atheist, who scorns religion because he has found no evidence for its tenets, and the believer, who attempts to prove the existence of God, have fallen victim to the "other"—to the idol-worship of the scientific style of thinking. Religious beliefs are not analogous to the scientific style of thinking, and should not be accepted or rejected using the same evidential criteria.[1]

The term "scientific" in the above text is referring to the classical causal and deterministic, realist viewpoint. Clearly there is a place for thinking in causal terms, but an absolute causality does not even apply to science (e.g., quantum). It is even further wrongheaded to set religious meaning in terms of causality. Just as a language matrix was shown as the nexus for scientific understanding, in contrast to epistemology and realism or, in other words, in contrast to one's mind or a strict material or mathematical foundation, the same argument applies to religion.

Realism and its flip side of nonrealism are problematic in philosophy and physics, and the same relates to religion. In order to see this,

---

[1] Ray Monk, *Ludwig Wittgenstein: The Duty of Genius* (London: Jonathan Cape, 1990). Wittgenstein, quoted in Monk, 410.

it is important to realize that science and religion are not competing for the best explanation of reality on the scientific realist's playing field. The essential reason for many thinking that science and religion are in a competition for the best explanation is that we are typically caught in the fly-bottle of realism, and then may easily conclude that science therefore offers the best objective explanations. However, as Dilman says: "When science is characterized as 'objective' this should not be understood as a word of praise; but it is often so understood—mistakenly. Certainly scientific truth is not the only kind of truth there is, scientific knowledge not the only kind of knowledge."[2] Moreover, Kerr writes:

> In our culture we are gripped by notions of explanation, proof, meaning, and truth that operate in the hard sciences, where we achieve marvelous things; yet, as Wittgenstein and Wisdom fear, we easily slip into assuming there really is no other way of using our minds, no other way of reaching rational decisions, no other way of reaching moral judgments; either they are objective or they are purely subjective, and that means irrational.[3]

Oddly, while atheist scientists may criticize theologians of being indoctrinated, they themselves are indoctrinated; in both cases the point being made in the following is not whether one is indoctrinated into atheism or religious belief. Rather, it is whether one is indoctrinated into realism, and, as Phillips says: "Theological non-realism is as empty as theological realism. Both terms are battle cries in a confused philosophical and theological debate."[4] Again, the common playing field is judged by a realist referee and most dialogue between science and religion plays on this conceptual field.

---

[2] Dilman, *Wittgenstein's Copernican Revolution*, 109.
[3] Kerr, *Work on Oneself*, 93.
[4] D. Z. Phillips, *Wittgenstein and Religion*, Swansea Studies in Philosophy (Basingstoke: Macmillan, 1993), 35.

Wittgenstein comments:

> Our craving for generality has another main source: our preoccupation with the method of science. I mean the method of reducing the explanation of natural phenomena to the smallest possible number of primitive natural laws; and in mathematics, of unifying the treatment of different topics by using a generalization. Philosophers constantly see the method of science before their eyes, and are irresistibly tempted to ask and answer questions in the way science does. This tendency is the real source of metaphysics, and leads the philosopher into complete darkness. I want to say here that it can never be our job ... to explain anything. Philosophy really *is* "purely descriptive".[5]

Of course, the method of science that Wittgenstein is referring to is that which is in line with classical physics. It is important to see that theologians and Christian scientists can certainly be included in the above when, as seems common, they set the science and religion dialogue within the context of current science. The language matrix is the nexus of reality, but this matrix, it should be clear, does not determine the one language or conception of reality. So, although science and religion fit in the logic of the matrix, they will have different concerns and thoughts. Yet what is similar between science and religion is that both frequently are stuck in the fly-bottle of realism and thereby miss the language matrix they are in.

For example, Wentzel van Huyssten says that theologians are "first and last theoreticians" who "construct theories in order to explain, as fully as possible, the hidden structures of the studied matter."[6] He thinks that religion, like science, should be progressive and account for an objective reality. In a similar fashion, Brian Hebblethwaite notes that "the most plausible hypothesis to account for this objectivity is a

---

[5] Wittgenstein, *Blue and Brown Books*, 18.
[6] In Andrew Moore, *Realism and the Christian Faith: God, Grammar, and Meaning* (Cambridge: Cambridge University Press, 2003), 45.

God."[7] In effect, he argues from an ontological idea of truth, then subsequently to God. Michael Banner, in *The Justification of Science and the Rationality of Religious Belief*, notes the importance of explanatory arguments along with Janet Soskice.[8] And Andrew Moore is clearly correct when he notes that Soskice and Arthur Peacocke regard religion to be, like science, in the business of theorizing.[9] The problem here is rightly seen by Rhees when he notes that conceiving of religion in the above terms confuses our conception of religion; the "trouble comes from thinking of Christianity and of belief in God as a kind of *theory*. And then it seems as though, if we were clear about it, it must be either science or pseudo-science."[10] Furthermore, Rhees says: "What I wish to bring out is: that the difficulties and barriers that separate those who are not religious from those who are—are not like the difficulties (say) that separated the views of Einstein and Niels Bohr ... The 'divide' is not a divide between two theories."[11] In other words, what separates the religious from the nonreligious is one's form of life, and this form of life is in the language matrix—which is not a competing theory.

What does it mean to have a religious form of life? A form of life that includes God? Do we gain knowledge of God through rational thought or sense experience? Despite the difference between rationalism and empiricism, they both base the container of knowledge as our mind, that is, ideas. Once again, this is the separation between our mind and the reality that is "out there." This is, unfortunately, the common basis for much discussion regarding God for the above scientists and theologians. One aspect of this thought begins with classical foundationalism, which maintains that some propositions are basic, that is, those with evidence, and therefore are

---

[7] Ibid., 16.
[8] Ibid., 29.
[9] Ibid., 44.
[10] Rhees, *Rush Rhees on Religion and Philosophy*, 127.
[11] Ibid., 129.

foundational. If a proposition is not basic, then as long as it can be traced back to a basic proposition then it can be accepted. From this it follows, as held in evidentalism, that propositions must be either self-evident (e.g., logical syllogism) or evident to our senses. This form of thought is then used to argue for the existence of God. For example, Locke notes:

> The visible marks of extraordinary Wisdom and Power, appear so plainly in all the Works of Creation, that a rational creature, who will but seriously reflect on them, cannot miss the discovery of a Deity ... it seems stranger to me, that a whole Nation of Men should be anywhere found so brutish, as to want the Notion of a God; than that they should be without any Notion of Numbers, or Fire.[12]

What Locke is doing here is using reason to conclude that God is the best explanation for the evidence. In contrast to the religious use of evidentalism—but still evidentalism—Bertrand Russell replied to the question of ending up in heaven in front of God—what would he say? "Sir, why did you not give me better evidence?"[13] So, the natural question to ask is: "Who has it right, Locke or Bertrand?" The correct answer is neither! Both show a misunderstanding of faith in God, that is, equating religious beliefs with empirical truth and focusing on the scientific method to justify or discredit belief in God. Yet, in terms of properly basic ideas based on empirical terms—if this is the exclusive method of determining reality—then Russell would be correct. Since evidentalism is how most atheists think religion works, they are thereby correct to reject religious beliefs. This form of thought should be rejected by theology, as Kerr notes: "Wittgenstein's lifelong objection to natural theology was that it purports to exhibit as the conclusion of an argument something that should have been manifest from the outset—if only we could see the world without demanding a

---

[12] Locke, *An Essay Concerning Human Understanding*, 89.
[13] Leo Rosten, "Bertrand Russell and God: A Memoir," *Saturday Review* (Feb. 23, 1974), 25–6.

certain kind of explanation."[14] It should be obvious that I am not saying there is no God; rather, evidentalism does not show that there is a God. The realist may say that "physical objects exist," but this is pointless; nonetheless, the realist thinks it is important so our language (or sense-experience) then has something to connect to, when in fact reality is in our language—which is why "physical objects exist" is not a proposition but a grammatical remark. This shows how the realist position is equated with their understanding of language.

However, there is an alternate to evidentalism, namely, Reformed epistemology—arguably the most well-known Christian philosophy of religion. It is nothing like classical physics, obviously, yet it follows a similar line of thought—that "things" can be fully explained on the basis of empirical evidence. Reformed epistemology rightly rejects both classical foundationalism and evidentalism. It sees the problem of trying to find a foundation, that is, the criterion of basicality simply cannot be sustained by self-evident propositions or sense experience. The intent is to avoid the problematic results of empiricism, that when using religious language it does not refer to a particular object. In this rejection of classical foundationalism and evidentalism, reformed epistemology is also rejecting atheist foundationalist claims that religious beliefs are false. In other words, neither the theist nor the atheist can claim the evidentalist foundational ground.

Nonetheless, reformed epistemology wants to secure a belief in God so the game is changed. Rather than searching for evidence, belief in God *is* foundational or, in other words, it is basic. So the evidentalist looks for objective evidence and rational arguments, while the reformed epistemologist says belief is basic. A reference is often made to John Calvin regarding this: "The knowledge of God has been naturally implanted in the human mind."[15] Even Descartes thinks that there are "primary seeds of truth naturally implanted in human

---

[14] Kerr, *Work on Oneself*, 49.
[15] Calvin, bk 1, ch. 3, sec. 1.

minds."[16] Given this universal noetic structure (reformed epistemology thinks sin can mask this knowledge), there is no need for evidence of God since belief in God is properly basic. So whereas the evidentalist uses logic and the senses to arrive at the conclusion that God must exist, the reformed epistemologist jumps straight to reason. Kerr rightly sees that Wittgenstein's "rejection of what he takes to be the strategy of founding faith upon rational demonstration leads him to regard faith as absolutely repellent to reason—'If Christianity is the truth then all the philosophy that is written about it is false.'"[17]

The problem here is that both evidentalists and reformed epistemologists do not initially consider the religious form of life; for the latter it is not basic, instead it is subsequent to a basic belief. This places basic belief as, to use Wittgenstein's terminology, a "primitive natural law." Paul Holmer remarks:

> The fact that Wittgenstein and other analytic logicians have made strong remarks about forms of life having an ultimacy has also created the notion that theology is like metaphysics in not being any longer the final court of justification. If forms of life are foundational, then it looks as though fideism is more crucial than theology. So it is that followers of Wittgenstein and Wittgenstein himself are assumed to be of the mind that denies that there is a recognizable kind of knowledge of God and that therefore theology is not truly cognitive, objective and rational. Oddly enough, Barthians, Kierkegaardians, and Wittgensteinians together look like the opponents of cognitivity and rationality in religion, but only if a certain pattern of rationality is taken to be normative.[18]

However, as Moore notes: "The fundamental epistemic stance of theological realists who intend to be faithful to Christian tradition is in fact fideistic."[19] In contrast to the realists, and as Wittgenstein

---

[16] Descartes, *The Philosophical Writings of Descartes*, 1:18.
[17] Kerr, Work on Oneself, 49. Wittgenstein, *Culture and Value*, 83.
[18] Paul Holmer, *The Grammar of Faith* (San Francisco: Harper & Row, 1978), 184.
[19] Moore, *Realism and the Christian Faith*, 58.

shows, a religious belief is tied to language and one's form of life; in other words, a language matrix. Religious belief is internal to the form of life—not external to it.

Thus, the problem, once again, is not between science and religion; it is a problem of realism in science and in religion. As noted previously, realist fundamentalism in science distorts and confuses the quantum, and the same applies to religion. These concepts are stuck in the fly-bottle and, as Wittgenstein says: "Concepts lead us to make investigations; are the expression of our interest, and direct our interest."[20] What becomes important in physics, which was not the case in classical physics, is the concept of the new grammar; where the grammar of the quantum is not set in a strict epistemological relation. The same applies to religion and its grammar. Moore says: "Against theological realists, I contend that their emphasis on theology's cognitive claims reflects a post-Enlightenment, foundationalist, and apologetic concern with epistemology."[21] Stating this problem of the theological realists does not require one to thereby conclude that there are no physical objects and that there is no God, as could be the conclusion of those stuck in the realist fly-bottle. On the contrary, it can lead us to a better understanding of God. It is actually the realist who loses reality in favor of a theory, while Wittgenstein gains reality in the language matrix. Moore rightly says: "Theological realists depict the represented in a way which makes it very hard to take it as more than anything 'more than the shadow or reflection of the representer.'"[22]

The realist may imagine that what I am saying can only lead to the conclusion that either everything is completely arbitrary or is an artifact in one's mind since there is no foundation of evidence or innate mind categories. However, as Phillips says: "We are tempted

---

[20] Wittgenstein, *Philosophical Investigations*, §570.
[21] Moore, *Realism and the Christian Faith*, 54.
[22] Ibid., 141.

to get behind what we do to something more fundamental, when what we need is a clarifying description of the place of concepts in our lives."[23] Moreover, as Kerr correctly notes, Wittgenstein saw that "religious practices have significance just as they are, and not because they are based on anything would-be scientific or theoretical or intellectual or metaphysical."[24] We do not need evidence or justification for the language matrix, and this does not mean that it is categorically arbitrary. As Paul Holmer remarks: "For just as grammar of a language is not quite an invention, nor do we simply make up our logical rules, so we do not design theology just to suit ourselves," rather, "the grammar of a language is that set of rules that describes how people speak that are doing it well and with efficacy."[25] Like quantum physics, where the calculations are exact, yet there is no determined connection to a foundational theory behind the calculations, the same applies to religion.

Norman Malcolm notes, regarding Wittgenstein's understanding of language compared to religion: "First, in both there is an end to explanation; second, in both there is an inclination to be amazed at the existence of something; third, into both there enters the notion of an 'illness'; fourth, in both, *doing, acting,* takes priority over the intellectual understanding and reasoning."[26] For example, as Malcolm says, "the word 'explanation' appears in many different language-games, and is used differently in different games ... An explanation is *internal* to a particular language-game. There is no explanation that *rises above* our language-games, and explains *them*. This would be a *super-concept* of explanation—which means that it is an ill-conceived fantasy."[27] The amazement is tied, as Wittgenstein himself

---

[23] Phillips, *Wittgenstein's On Certainty*, 146.
[24] Kerr, *Work on Oneself*, 52.
[25] Holmer, *Grammar of Faith*, 20.
[26] Norman Malcolm, *Wittgenstein: A Religious Point of View?*, ed. Peter Winch (New York: Cornell University Press, 1995), 92.
[27] Malcolm, *Wittgenstein*, 77–8.

says, to language itself: "Let your self be struck by the existence of the language-games."²⁸ The illness is seeking beyond our language, as Wittgenstein states:

> A remarkable and characteristic phenomena in philosophical investigation: the difficulty—I might say—is not that of finding the solution but rather of recognizing as the solution something that looks as if it were only preliminary to it ... This is connected, I believe, with our wrongly expecting an explanation, if we give it the right place in out considerations. If we dwell upon it, and do not try to get beyond it. The difficulty here is: to stop.²⁹

The basic problem of considering grammar to be a description of "reality" independent of our physical existence is found, for example, in the idea that there is a complete conception of reality to be discovered, a theory of everything or, in the case of theology, perhaps we do not yet have complete understanding but surely God does. This basic idea can follow one of two roads: "down" to the most basic elements as a foundation or "up" to a metaphysical theory.

However, Kerr remarks:

> We don't proceed from supposed primitive elements to construct entities. It's very simple really. The choice lies between Newton and Goethe; between atomism and holism; between supposing that what is fundamental is elements that you get down to by analysis and supposing that what is fundamental is what you see on the face of things right at the start. To believe that you get more deeply into what things or people are, by analyzing them into their constituent parts and putting the bits together again, is an illusion.³⁰

Just as the quantum does not allow a determined and discrete collection of "things" to be built on, neither does God fit into such an

---

[28] Wittgenstein, *Philosophical Investigations*, §224.
[29] Wittgenstein, *Zettel*, §314.
[30] Kerr, *Work on Oneself*, 66.

analysis. Certainly, we may not be trying to work out the discrete components of God, but we might try to demarcate God through metaphysical categories such as omnipotent, impassible, etc.; or in the case of physics proceed on a similar path to the multiverse or a mathematical universe. In all these cases there is a search for uniformity that is external to language; in other words, realism.

It is interesting to note an obvious but rarely considered thought of Richard Feynman: "The atoms that are in the brain are being replaced: the ones that were there before have gone away. So what is this mind of ours: what are these atoms with consciousness? Last week's potatoes! ... The thing I call my individuality is only a pattern or a dance."[31] Whatever a person thinks of the physical world, it is not a determinate physical base; instead, reality is based on the unity of language and life together as the language matrix. The point is not that a potato is the same as your brain, obviously not! Yet they are the same—and interchangeable—at the most elemental level. What does this show? That our reality cannot be reduced to an ultimate physical base. The fact that we are not physically the same person from one moment to the next shows that at the bottom a reductionist explanation does not work. More central to life is information, which continues in the stream of life in contrast to particular particles. Language carries this information in the continuity in life, and it is what individuates us, since it is clearly not the case, at the most elementary level, that we are distinct. Zeilinger notes Pauli writing in a letter to Markus Fierz: "That which is physically unique cannot be separated from the observer anymore—and therefore falls through the net of physics. The individual case is the occasion and causa. I am inclined to see in this 'occasio'—which includes the observer and his choice of the experimental setup and procedure—a 'revenue' of

---

[31] Feynman, *What Do You Care What Other People Think*, 244.

the 'anima mundi' (of course in 'changed shape') that was pushed aside in the 17th century."[32]

Bohr notes that it is important "further to explore the situation as regards analysis and synthesis in quantum physics and its analogies in other fields of human knowledge, where customary terminology implies attention to the conditions under which experience is gained."[33] Classical grammar is used to describe the measurement. Whereas the surface grammar of the quantum is statistical and about abstract entities, and the various rules of the quantum world, this does not show the relation between the quantum and our everyday world. This is indeed the surface grammar of the quantum, but it does not get to the depth grammar (recall the distinction between principles of logic and the logic of language) of how it works in our everyday world, and we know it does! Quantum physics cannot deal exclusively with the surface grammar of the quantum and the application of the quantum without working out the depth grammar of the quantum. The language used regarding the quantum does not include the grammar of objects, just as the language of mathematics does not include the grammar of objects. But does this mean it is meaningless? No! Is the language of justice and love meaningless? Rather than emphasizing the abstract or virtual particles, the emphasis should be on the grammar of the quantum and how it is used.

The point is to show that the surface grammar of abstraction can lead us away from its use, in other words, away from application to metaphysics. Grammar is our reality, and propositions make claims within this reality. The question "do numbers exist?" makes little sense in the abstract; however, when calculating one works with numbers and understands what they are. Likewise, in the quantum world it makes little sense to ask if x, y, z particles exist; instead, we should see

---

[32] Zeilinger, "On the Interpretation and Philosophical Foundations of Quantum Mechanics," 173.
[33] Bohr, *Essays 1958–1962 on Atomic Physics and Human Knowledge*, Vol. III, 93.

the use of this category of particles in calculations and experiments. Wittgenstein would say language is "idling" when it is not working. To know if the temperature of water in a beaker is above 5 degrees Celsius we measure the temperature, but in the case of God and the wave function there is already a set of conditions, and if there is any disagreement it thereby follows that it is a difference in grammar, not one of a simple measurement. The point here is that there is a different grammar at work.

Rules of grammar contrast with empirical rules in the following manner. If I want to fix a piston ring in my engine there are certain rules to follow. However, note that whatever goal one works toward, it is through language, and it is grammar that provides the context. This context itself is not questioned and requires no explanation, unlike the propositions in the empirical world describing a particular state of affairs. What enables a proposition, which could be true or false, is its grammar. Reality is information, verified instants, measurements, and our language—within these is the quantum and grammar. As Wittgenstein notes: "Logical inference is a transition that is justified if it follows a particular paradigm, and whose rightness is not dependent on anything else."[34] What is independent of language is not reality, it is objects in reality. Moreover, to say "'A is a physical object' is a piece of instruction which we give to someone who doesn't yet understand either what 'A' means or what 'physical object' means. Thus it is instruction about the use of words, and 'physical object' is a logical concept. (Like color, quantity . . .) And that is why no such proposition as 'There are physical objects' can be formulated."[35]

Given these thoughts, it is useful to quote Rush Rhees at length:

We use "it exists" chiefly in connection with physical objects, and anyway we use it where we can ask whether it exists or not. This goes with

---

[34] Wittgenstein, *Remarks on the Foundations of Mathematics*, part 5, 45.
[35] Wittgenstein, *On Certainty*, §36.

the sense of *finding out* whether it exists. Now the "it", whatever it is, is something we could identify in such an investigation—by, for example, the methods by which we commonly identify a particular physical object. We might also confuse it with something else, or mistake something for it. But in any case, the question *whether* it was the same object would involve those sorts of criteria. But the question whether we mean the same by "God", I have said, is not a question whether we are referring to the same object. The question whether we are still talking about God now, or whether we are really worshipping God now, cannot be settled by referring to any object. And I do not think it would mean anything to ask "whether any such object exists". Nor does it change anything if you say "being" instead of "object".[36]

What is the objective reality of God? God as an independent reality, on the basis of a physical object, is a confused notion. This does not mean that there is no God; rather, it means that it is a confused way of speaking about God. Perhaps God is not a physical object to be discussed, but is the quanta? It is only as shown that we are able to discern, in the case of God this is the Word, and in the case of the quantum it is the particle. The confusion arises when we assume that there is one language and one grammar for it. But if we realize that one is the grammar of the quanta (in and of itself) and the other classical (the specific measurement) and the two are distinct, then we do not need to try and reconcile them. Granted, I am not saying there are multiple realities; rather, the quantum is rules (not empirical), whereas particle position is empirical. As Wittgenstein notes: "Grammar tells what kind of object anything is. (Theology as grammar.)"[37]

Since particles do not have a determined position or momentum until measured, yet once measured they are physical objects with, in the case of a measurement of position, a resultant position, it follows that the quantum world is a world of grammar until a measurement

---

[36] Rush Rhees, "Religion and Language," *Without Answers* (London: Routledge & Kegan Paul, 1969), 131.
[37] Wittgenstein, *Philosophical Investigations*, §373.

is made; at which point we can have a proposition regarding the location. Note that reality and grammar go hand in hand, and reality is *in* the grammar, the grammar does not refer to reality. In other words, the point has been that what is internal to language is reality—not a particular particle that may or may not exist. Instead, what is internal to language is grammar, the realm within which we can say a particle is here or there once measured.

The reality of the quantum world is not the question; instead, we question aspects of that reality. What specifically exists or does not exist is not *in* the grammar; instead, the grammar is the realm within which a particle exists. The grammatical is not questioned as to whether it does or does not exist, only that within it is questioned. Thus, there is a circularity between our grammar and reality. For example, a proposition may say that a particle hit the plate at this spot. That particle and where it hit are independent of language. Yet how is this context understood? Well, it is a proposition about a particle hitting the plate. More specifically, the grammar of the proposition, which itself is neither true nor false, is internal to the proposition. So, the measurement fixes a particular particle, and the grammar fixes the reality to which the proposition is directed. This is the two-way relationship between language and reality.

Likewise, we do not decide that there is or is not a God, as Rhees notes: "If it were like that, the question would not have the importance it has."[38] Grammar in relation to reality, like God in relation to reality, is not physical object language, and is not true or false by checking the state of affairs. Reality is often thought of as things to which language refers in the world, and thus makes some sense to us, but, remember as noted earlier, reality here is being argued as directly tied to language and how our activities and form of life are intertwined. What is the relation of logic to reality? Or perhaps more concretely mathematics to reality? Are they real? To answer this is not to answer

[38] Rhees, *Rush Rhees on Religion and Philosophy*, 153.

in terms of physical objects. Instead, these are shown in the way we live. Likewise, the reality of God is not provided through scientific or physical object investigation; instead it is based on our form of life. Yet, as is the case for language (to abate the realists' alarm here), we do not simply create, willy-nilly, logic, mathematics, and God. The problem does not reside in potential worries regarding relativism and arbitrariness; rather, it resides with the idea that we need to seek foundations to justify logic, mathematics, and God.

Both science (at least traditionally) and religion gravitate toward object language, but as shown this is problematic. However, if object language is left behind, then an equally problematic mathematical or abstract metaphysical illusion is happy to take its place. The problem of, for example, the multiverse, is that it is simply the flip side of the former object determinism—just an abstract variant. Rather than flying off toward theories such as the multiverse, it is useful to stop at the mystery. Energy-matter is like Wittgenstein's "form of life": the former is tied to information we measure and the latter the language we use. Since there is no cause-effect determined understanding of a particle, it then follows that probabilities are the rule (unless one thinks the wave function never collapses, etc.). Yet there is a determined measure that is certain. Is it right to then focus on the probabilities? This is still a reductionism. To assume that this leads to complete arbitrariness is to have the preconception that it is absolutely necessary that everything be predetermined. Instead, the emphasis should shift from the seed structure to the plant, which in and of itself is not probable.

Randomness is not at the bottom of the system, it is in the system. In a sense, this is an irreducible mystery, not unlike what Zeilinger says: "We remark that this kind of randomness must then be irreducible, that is, it cannot be reduced to hidden properties of the system."[39] Philosophers, particularly of the past, were too eager to find metaphysical foundations, and scientists too eager to find a reductionist

---

[39] Zeilinger, "A Foundational Principle for Quantum Mechanics," 636.

foundation, all looking beyond language and the form of life. Yet our everyday life is uniform. Wittgenstein says: "Thinking and inferring (like counting) is of course bounded for us, not by an arbitrary definition, but by natural limits corresponding to the body of what can be called the role of thinking and inferring in our life."[40] Only within a form of religious life can one ask if *x, y, z*, is true or false. In this sense the grammar is not arbitrary (as some may assume since it is not founded on an a priori foundation external to it), and the quantum propositions and the rules of calculations are not arbitrary, since they are applied in our lives.

Because of tendencies toward realism and foundationalism, when faced with randomness and fluidity, the assumption is that it cannot be; how can we have a proper causal relation if at the bottom the cause is random? Once again, as Einstein famously said: "God does not play dice." The problem here is realism, causality, and epistemology. In describing our world and living in our world, are we concerned that suddenly one's house will disappear? The quantum is not an external foundation of reality, it is in reality. Or, for another example, take a black hole and time stopping, are we then afraid that at some point, time will stop during our day? The latter example is obviously not discussed among various debates compared to the quantum example (e.g., Schrödinger's cat). The reason for discussions of the strange behavior of the quantum and its problematic introduction to our everyday world is a reductionistic one, because we assume the smallest parts are the ultimate basis of reality and form our reality.

There is a link between the pursuit of a determinate system in physics, mathematical beauty, and God, as unchanging categories. In particular, the classical view of God is very transcendent, separate from fluctuating nature and thereby actually approaching deism. Once again, classical theism commonly promotes the impassible nature of God, basically meaning that God does not change. It may

---

[40] Wittgenstein, *Remarks on the Foundations of Mathematics*, Vol. I, 116.

not be apparent at first, but this is similar to typical classical thoughts regarding the physical world, that it is "out there" and we are separate from it. Even if one applies lofty terminology, such as "omniscient, impassible," etc. to God, there remains the mystery of the loftiness of these categories—who can extend their knowledge far enough into these mysteries? In other words, the depth of being impassible can theoretically be understood—it is just that we do not currently (if ever) have the ability to do so. Therefore, the depth of impassibility remains a mystery. In contrast to such thoughts, the mystery of God is not an epistemological mystery. If it were, then we may be tempted to assume that *that* reality, namely, God's reality, is what is true, while we are in the shadows. Wittgenstein says: "It is very *remarkable* that we should be inclined to think of civilization—houses, trees, cars, etc.— as separating man from his origins, from what is lofty and eternal, etc. Our civilized environment, along with its trees and plants, strikes us then as though it were cheaply wrapped in cellophane and isolated from everything great, from God, as it were. That is a remarkable picture that intrudes on us."[41] Note that there is a parallel thought in terms of the multiverse and a mathematical universe. In both cases, our world and form of life, the language matrix is bypassed in favor of theories that reach out to epistemological abstractions.

What if God and the quantum are a mystery—but not an epistemological mystery? Neither the particle nor a proposition capture the entire wave function or language; we rest on the limit and see the form shown in the statistical probabilities and grammar. It is not, in quantum physics, simply the case that causes are unknown and therefore currently a mystery; instead, there are no causes. Likewise, God is a mystery not because there is something we do not yet understand, but because God is a mystery. Moreover, we cannot delve into grammar and force it to conform to whatever we want; it is a mystery. It is important to understand that the mystery does not mean that we have

---

[41] Wittgenstein, *Culture and Value*, 50.

an understanding up to a certain limit and then fail to get further; rather it is part of our understanding of God. This is not an epistemological problem, it is a conceptual understanding. As Wittgenstein says: "Perhaps what is inexpressible (what I find mysterious and am not able to express) is the background against which whatever I could express has its meaning."[42] Or, as Bohr notes: "In quantum mechanics, we are not dealing with an arbitrary renunciation of a more detailed analysis of atomic phenomena, but with a recognition that such an analysis is in principle excluded."[43]

Likewise, Kierkegaard says:

> Suppose Christianity to be a mystery and intentionally so, a genuine and not a theatrical mystery, which is revealed in the fifth act of the drama, while a clever spectator sees through it in the course of the exposition. Suppose that a revelation ... must be a mystery, and that its sole and sufficient mark is precisely that it is a mystery ... Suppose it were after all a blessed thing, critically situated in the extreme press of existence, to sustain a relation to this mystery without understanding it, merely as a believer. Suppose Christianity never intended to be understood; suppose that, in order to express this, and to prevent anyone from misguidedly entering upon the objective way, it has declared itself to be a paradox ... Suppose it refuses to be understood and that the maximum of understanding which could come in question is to understand that it cannot be understood.[44]

Another way of looking at this is the following. If we could potentially have all the information of a system and all the information of God, then would this entail, in a sense, the destruction of our reality? Would everything stop? I do not mean *once* we knew everything it

---

[42] Ibid., 16.
[43] In Arkady Plotnitsky, "Mysteries without Mysticism and Correlations without Correlata: On Quantum Knowledge and Knowledge in General," *Foundations of Physics*, 33, no. 11 (2003), 1651.
[44] Søren Kierkegaard, *Concluding Unscientific Postscript*, trans. David Swenson, completed after his death; introduction and notes by Walter Lowrie (Princeton, NJ: Princeton University Press, 1974), 191.

would stop; rather, such a state would be immovable. Thus, could we then say that the paradox is necessary for our reality?

In science the importance of measurement is clear, and our concepts play a key role in the relationship between what we decide to measure and our understanding of the measurement. Yet what the experiments show, according to the Copenhagen interpretation, is that the quantum is a mystery. All we can say is that this is a description of the result of measurements, and that a specific measurement shows the associated specific data, while a different measurement could have produced a different result. That is the reality of our grammar (rules) of the quantum, and it enables incredibly accurate calculations. Likewise, Wittgenstein remarks:

> Language is an instrument. Its concepts are instruments. Now perhaps one thinks that it can make no *great* difference *which* concepts we employ. As, after all, it is possible to do physics in feet and inches as well as in metres and centimetres; the difference is merely one of convenience. But even this is not true if, for instance, calculations in some system of measurement demand more time and trouble than it is possible for us to give them.[45]

In other words, our language as an instrument is directly tied to our concepts, and this forms our understanding of reality; we are participants. As Dilman says: "Our language is not founded on an empirical reality with which we are in contact through sense perception. Rather it is our language, conceived as part of our life and our life as a life of the language we speak that determines the kind of contact we have with such a reality in our conception of it insofar as we live its life."[46] Moreover, Polkinghorne notes that "there is a kind of epistemological circle: how we know an entity must conform to the nature of that entity; the nature of the entity is revealed

---

[45] Wittgenstein, *Philosophical Investigations*, §569.
[46] Dilman, *Wittgenstein's Copernican Revolution*, 10.

through what we know about it. There can be no escape from this delicate circularity."⁴⁷ We are part of the system, we are participants, and this, in quantum physics, is a necessary part of information, and the same applies to religion; information is found in an objectivity outside observers.

Yet the practice of religion is frequently not seen as important. Moore rightly notes that the arguments of theological realism "lead them to construe 'God' in terms drawn from the philosophy of science rather than from its role in Christian activities such as prayer and worship."⁴⁸ This is the case in reformed epistemology where the search for knowledge and justification leads to an assumed innate knowledge of God, and subsequently practices follow. In such a case Wittgenstein would say: "We have got on to slippery ice where there is no friction and so in a certain sense the conditions are ideal, but also, just because of that, we are unable to walk. We want to walk: so we need friction. Back to the rough ground!"⁴⁹ Hence, Wittgenstein notes: "How are we taught the word 'God' (its use that is)? I cannot give a full grammatical description of it. But I can, as it were, make some contributions to such a description; I can say a good deal about it and perhaps in time assemble a sort of collection of examples."⁵⁰ Descriptions are directly linked to the "instrument" of language in terms of practices, rather than theories and elaborate explanations regarding things such as a noetic seed implanted in one's brain. Kerr rightly says that "Wittgenstein is doing his utmost to protect the mystery of the human soul; –but against the 'Cartesian' or 'Protestant' picture of the soul as radically private, the inner light, the secret self, the hidden conscience or whatever, Wittgenstein takes what I am sure he never realized is the essentially Catholic

---

⁴⁷ Polkinghorne, *Quantum Theory*, 87.
⁴⁸ Moore, *Realism and Christian Faith*, 75.
⁴⁹ Wittgenstein, *Philosophical Investigations*, §107.
⁵⁰ Wittgenstein, *Culture and Value*, 82.

line: there is no experience, so there is no experience of God either, which is not mediated."[51]

So, what are the descriptions? The mediation? The answer is the practices. As Rhees says: "You cannot have the idea of God apart from religious worship. You could not explain to anyone what we mean by 'God' without pointing to all that belongs to religious worship."[52] Moreover, as Martin Luther says, whoever

> wants to find Christ, must first find the church. How would one know Christ and [have] faith in him if one did not know where they are who believe in him? He who would know something concerning Christ, must neither trust in himself nor build his bridge into heaven by means of his own reason, but he should go to church ... The church is not wood and stone but the assembly of people who believe in Christ. With this church one should be connected and see how the people believe, live, and teach.[53]

Clearly, this would seem unsatisfactory to the realist who would then go further and ask how this is justified and how one knows that these things connect to a God. These questions clearly miss the relationship between the participant and God, which is mediated in these practices. As Rhees notes:

> In Christianity one's relation to God *is* the worship of God ... if anyone should ask what the relation of the creature to God is, then one might most readily point to the worship of God, as if to say: "Look there, you'll see." And this is not the sort of thing that is suggested by Plato's idea of becoming as like to the divine as possible. Indeed, it could be said it is just the opposite. When Plato speaks of the form of the good ... he does not say that the sensible world, and earthly life, is any sort of imitation or likeness of that.[54]

---

[51] Kerr, *Work on Oneself*, 58.
[52] Rhees, *Rush Rhees on Religion and Philosophy*, 199.
[53] Martin Luther, "The Gospel for the Early Christmas Service," in *Luther's Works: Sermons II, American Edition*, ed. Hans J. Hillerbrand (Minneapolis, MN: Fortress Press, 1974), 39–40, 52.
[54] Rhees, *Rush Rhees on Religion and Philosophy*, 181.

In contrast to metaphysical theories and categories for God, and abstract theories beyond measurements in physics, the relation of the participant is essential in the language matrix. As Kerr realizes:

> It is the sin of angelism that Jacques Maritain located in Descartes, who "turned knowledge and thought into a hopeless perplexity, in an abyss of unrest, because he conceived human thought after the type of angelic thought." Against this seductive picture Wittgenstein simply reminds us that our inner life, our intellectual and spiritual inwardness, depends on a great variety of simple, natural, original inclinations on our part, culturally expressed and communicated, but requiring no grounding in anything supposedly deeper.[55]

Given this, Wittgenstein rightly notes that "Christianity is not a doctrine, not, I mean, a theory about what has happened and will happen to the human soul, but a description of something that actually takes place in human life. For 'consciousness of sin' is a real event and so are despair and salvation through faith."[56] Kierkegaard notes the problem of the lack of this relationship: "Most systematizers in relation to their systems are like a man who builds an enormous castle and himself lives alongside it in a shed; they themselves do not live in the enormous systematic building. But in the realm of mind and spirit this nonresidence is and remains a decisive objection. Spiritually understood, a man's thoughts must be the building in which he lives—otherwise the whole thing is deranged."[57] The aforementioned realist theories fit Kierkegaard's criticism as they leave the language matrix in favor of what they regard as more essential and fundamental, namely, the use of reason to first justify belief in God rather than observing the belief in God in a particular instance. Just as the observer and the measurements form meaning regarding the quantum, in a sense the quantum reveals itself in the experiments,

---

[55] Kerr, *Work on Oneself*, 56.
[56] Wittgenstein, *Culture and Value*, 28.
[57] Kierkegaard, *Journals and Papers*, 519.

so is the case with God and the individual, where this participatory relationship, rather than a theory, shows God. There is frequently a wrongheaded thought that this implies some form of subjectivism or emotivism. As Phillips says, theological realists cannot take this relationship seriously "because for them, anything called an affective state or an attitude is merely a consequence of a belief said to be logically independent of it."[58] Yet, as noted by Kerr: "Wittgenstein sought to highlight the primacy of practice over intellect in religion, rather than that of feeling."[59] To assume that religious practices and the complementary relationship to God is simply subjective is clearly the result of a realist perspective. Rhees aptly notes Mikhail Bakunin's comment to Wittgenstein: " 'If God really existed, it would be necessary to abolish him'. And Wittgenstein said that at any rate this made more sense than did Voltaire's 'If there were not a God, it would be necessary to invent one'. The idea of 'inventing God' makes no sense at all."[60] Obviously, there may be cases where a subjectivist criticism could be applied, but it is wrong to apply this criticism universally. Indeed, to apply it universally necessarily entails a presupposition that there is no God. A similar line of thought applies to skepticism. Just because in one instance it has been right to be skeptical, it does not imply an absolute skepticism.

Religion and science need to see the importance of the language matrix, that is, rejecting both realism and nonrealism, placing language and information as central rather than one's mind or an external reality, and noting the essential aspect of participation. Despite the different contexts this is the principle for both. Moreover, there is a respective certainty in terms of belief and, for example, mathematical truths, as Wittgenstein says: "Unshakable faith. (e.g., in a promise.) Is it any less certain than being convinced of a mathematical

---

[58] Phillips, *Wittgenstein and Religion*, 47.
[59] Kerr, *Work on Oneself*, 53.
[60] Wittgenstein, "Wittgenstein's Philosophical Conversations with Rush Rhees," 56.

truth)—But does that make the language-games any more alike!"[61] Given these similarities for science and religion, there is nonetheless a clear difference. A key difference is revelation. This marks a difference in kind between religion and science. Alister McGrath rightly notes: "The theologian is unable to appeal to present experimentation, or the results of past experimentation ... Whereas the scientific community takes its ideas from such experimental approaches, the religious community takes them from revelation."[62]

It is significant to realize that while science may proceed on the basis of a hypothesis and experiment, religion does not—it is based on revelation. However, as should be clear, realist theologians often proceed to argue as if religion begins with a hypothesis and then concludes, given sufficient arguments, with the existence of God. Then, once again, worship can follow. In a sense, revelation is antithetical to realism. It strips the hypothesis, theories, and abstract creations. Wittgenstein's friend Drury remarked: "When say, Plato talks about the gods, it lacks that sense of awe which you feel throughout the Bible—from Genesis to Revelation. 'But who may abide the day of his coming, and who shall stand when he appeareth?'; Wittgenstein, 'standing still and looking at me very intently,' replied: 'I think you have just said something very important. Much more important than you realize.'"[63]

In religion, revelation makes a difference in one's life, unlike, for example, mathematics. Granted, mathematics has enabled all sorts of new things in our life, but the manner in which we relate to these things is different. Rhees says: "There is no difference between understanding ... mathematics and accepting mathematics. But there does seem to be a difference between understanding

---

[61] Wittgenstein, *Culture and Value*, 73.
[62] Alister McGrath, *The Foundations of Dialogue in Science and Religion* (Oxford: Blackwell, 1998), 206.
[63] M. O'C Drury, "Conversations with Wittgenstein," in *Recollections of Wittgenstein*, ed. Rush Rhees (Oxford: Oxford University Press, 1984), 161.

a religious doctrine and accepting a religious doctrine; and even between understanding the liturgy and the rest of a religious faith, and accepting that faith."[64] In the case of religion, one can understand, in a basic sense, the language. Indeed, an atheist could theoretically study theology and be well versed in theology but not believe any of it. Granted, someone may in general understand the Copenhagen interpretation, but not accept it. However, whether it is accepted or not does not make a significant difference in their daily life. The physicist's life is the same, albeit with a different conception of reality, whether or not one thinks John Bell's inequalities necessitates the rejection of local realism. However, belief in God is not a statement of fact, or accepting that a hypothesis is correct; instead, it is a confession and a relationship. In reply to Heisenberg, Bohr said: "Epistemological sophistries cannot possibly help him attain these ends (dealing with life, death, existence ...). Here, too, the relationship between critical thought about the spiritual content of a given religion and action based on the deliberate acceptance of that content is complementary."[65]

This relationship is shown in Malcolm's note, that Wittgenstein was "prepared by his own character and experience to comprehend the idea of a judging and redeeming God"; yet "any cosmological conception of a Deity, derived from the notions of cause or infinity, would be repugnant to him."[66] Indeed, Kerr says that Wittgenstein was "delighted when Malcolm quoted Kierkegaard: 'How can it be that Christ does not exist, since I know that He has saved me?' Wittgenstein replied: 'You see! It isn't a question of proving anything!'"[67] How can you argue that God loves you, when the other person believes that there is no God? It makes no sense to have an argument to prove God exists and then the person subsequently believes that God loves them.

---

[64] Rhees, *Rush Rhees on Religion and Philosophy*, 197.
[65] Heisenberg, *Physics and Beyond*, 90.
[66] Norman Malcolm, *Ludwig Wittgenstein: A Memoir* (Oxford: Clarendon Press, 2001), 59.
[67] Kerr, *Work on Oneself*, 48.

Rather, as Bohr noted, there is a complementary relationship between the spiritual and one's life.

There is a participatory nature in understanding the quantum, and there is a participatory nature in religion; indeed, Luther's remark may surprise many, namely, "faith creates the deity."[68] Clearly this shows the interrelationship between language and reality. Of course, Luther considers God to be the one who creates us rather than the opposite. Yet it is all too easy to be stuck in realism and therefore miss his deep point, namely, God is not simply a foundational object or a theory. The complementary revelation relationship is unique because it is with a person, as Lennox notes, "God is a person, not a theory."[69] Hence, Polkinghorne says:

> Like my fellow scientist-theologians, I have operated in a science-led mode. For example, I have written about natural theology, using the deep intelligibility of the universe and the finely tuned fruitfulness of its history as guides to the organization of the argument. As a quantum physicist, I have been concerned with understanding God's relationship to the physical universe. Yet I have also wanted to make clear, as opportunity offered, that the central source of my own belief in God does not lie in such matters. Rather, it is to be found in my encounter with the figure of Jesus Christ, as I meet him in scripture, in the Church and in the sacraments.[70]

In Christianity, "God," "Jesus Christ," and the "Word" (*Logos*) are inseparable, yet the terms refer to different natures of God, with the latter two being the mark of revelation—being shown. God is the *Deus abscondicus* (God hidden), while Jesus Christ is the *Deus revelatatus* (God revealed). As Hermann Sasse notes: "God is hidden when he reveals Himself in Christ."[71] This is like the quantum and the particle.

---

[68] Luther, *Luther's Works*, 26, 227.
[69] Lennox, *God and Stephen Hawking*, 94.
[70] John C. Polkinghorne, *Science and the Trinity: The Christian Encounter with Reality* (New Haven, CT: Yale University Press, 2004), xiii.
[71] Hermann Sasse, *We Confess Jesus Christ* (St. Louis: Concordia, 1984), 49.

The particle is in the measurement, the divine is in the flesh, and logic is in our language. In each case, the complementary and participatory relation makes these a reality.

An obvious comparison can then be made with Weizsacker's aforementioned remark that "objects are not *behind* phenomena, but *in* phenomena." As previously noted, God is not an object, yet God is an object in the Word; and as Ronald Hustwit notes Kierkegaard saying: "The Unknown is revealed in the known."[72] The use of the term "in" is not a coincidence; instead, it shows the nature of the relationships, in contrast to terms such as "from," "behind," or "above." The reason is that such terms would fit better in realism and would thereby displace the mystery. This mystery is not, as previously noted, an epistemological mystery of God or the quantum. Einstein's remark shows the mystery of the hidden revealed and the revealed as hidden:

> But what is light really? Is it a wave or a shower of photons? There seems no likelihood for forming a consistent description of the phenomena of light by a choice of only one of the two languages. It seems as though we must use sometimes the one theory and sometimes the other, while at times we may use either. We are faced with a new kind of difficulty. We have two contradictory pictures of reality; separately neither of them fully explains the phenomena of light, but together they do.[73]

In neither science nor religion is this mystery to be taken as mysticism, as Arkady Plotnitsky notes: "Bohr's interpretation of quantum mechanics as complementarity ... allows one to associate with it a certain mystery, this mystery is a mystery without mysticism."[74]

---

[72] Ronald E. Hustwit, *Something about O. K. Bouwsma* (Lanham, MD: University Press of America, 1992), 18.
[73] Albert Einstein and Leopold Infeld, *The Evolution of Physics* (New York: Simon & Schuster, 1966), 262–3.
[74] Plotnitsky, "Mysteries without Mysticism and Correlations without Correlata," 1651.

Instead, this mystery is a paradox, and as Heisenberg says: "The Copenhagen interpretation of quantum theory starts from a paradox."[75] Moreover, Zeilinger comments:

> It may very well be said that information is the irreducible kernel from which everything else flows. Then the question why nature appears quantized is simply a consequence of the fact that information itself is quantized by necessity. It might even be fair to observe that the concept that information is fundamental is very old knowledge of humanity, witness for example the beginning of gospel according to John: "In the beginning was the Word."[76]

Theology, particularly classical theism, frequently focuses on a transcendent God, which is, once again, comparable to physicists focusing on theories such as the multiverse. However, what we have, namely, the shown information and the Word, are taken as signposts to "something" else. Rather than signposts, they are the given, and are understood through the language matrix. As Peter Winch says: "God's reality is certainly independent of what any man may care to think, but what that reality amounts to can only be seen from the religious tradition in which the concept of God is used, … It is within the religious use of language that the concept of God's reality has a place."[77] Moreover, Bohr notes:

> Altogether, the approach towards the problem of explanation that is embodied in the notion of complementarity suggests itself in our position as conscious beings and recalls forcefully the teaching of ancient thinkers that, in the search for a harmonious attitude towards

---

[75] Werner Heisenberg, *Physics and Philosophy: The Revolution in Modern Science* (1958; Amherst, NY: Prometheus Books, 1999), 44.
[76] Anton Zeilinger, "Why the Quantum? It from Bit? A Participatory Universe? Three Far-Reaching, Visionary Questions from John Archibald Wheeler and How They Inspired a Quantum Experimentalist," presentation by Zeilinger at a symposium: "Science and Ultimate Reality: Celebrating the Vision of John Archibald Wheeler and Taking It Forward into a New Century of Discovery," Princeton University, March 2002.
[77] Winch, *Ethics and Action*, 12.

life, it must never be forgotten that we ourselves are both actors and spectators in the drama of existence. To such an utterance applies, of course, as well as to most of the sentences in this article from the beginning to the end, the recognition that our task can only be to aim at communicating experiences and views to others by means of language, in which the practical use of every word stands in a complementary relation to attempts of its strict definition.[78]

It is clear that for Christianity the text, that which is uniquely the Word in language form, is an important part of the communication of the tradition. Yet its nature can be misunderstood in a typical detached realist manner. For example, Sasse notes that to think "that an inspired writing must also be free from the least error ... [is] nothing more than an axiom like the axioms of Euclidian geometry."[79] There is often a desire to make the text a foundational authority that is external to human contamination (as God is thought of as being impassible).

Kevin Vanhoozer considers language and our form of life to be too arbitrary to support the burden of carrying the *truth*, and therefore places this burden on the text itself. He says his point is to "correct ... this cultural-linguistic misstep by locating authority not in the use of scripture by the believing community but what Nicholas Wolterstorff calls divine authorial discourse."[80] His goal is to get back to a foundational authority, whereby the text takes precedent over any relations to our lives and therefore it precedes the religious community.[81] This emphasis on the text, perhaps an ontological emphasis, is particularly odd—unless he thinks there is an ontological copy that predates

---

[78] Bohr, "On the Notions of Causality and Complementarity," 54.
[79] Hermann Sasse, *Scripture and the Church: Selected Essays of Hermann Sasse*, Concordia Seminary Monograph Series, no. 2, ed. Jeffrey J. Kloha and Ronald R. Feuerhahn (Chelsea, MI: BookCrafters, 1995), 154.
[80] Kevin Vanhoozer, *The Drama of Doctrine: A Canonical-Linguistic Approach to Christian Theology* (Louisville, KY: Westminster John Knox Press, 2005), 11.
[81] Ibid., 294.

religion. Moreover, how is anyone supposed to understand this text if not within a religious form of life? Like the reformed epistemologists' assumption, there must be some innate ability of reason on its own accord to realize that there is such a text and understand it, to then subsequently form a community from it.

In contrast, Rhees correctly notes that "the Bible itself was the outcome of religion before it was the source of it."[82] The text is not providing knowledge about the empirical world or knowledge of that which is beyond the world that a community then adopts. In other words, the text is not dropped into a community; instead, it is an account of the living Word which was in the community. The participants with the Word are central. As Sasse says, in terms of inspiration, that what was revealed was "in their language and in their conceptual world."[83] Consequently, Luther remarks:

> Tell me what language has there ever been that men have successfully learned to speak as a result of grammatical rules? Are not rather those languages that adhere most closely to rules, such as Greek and Latin, nevertheless learned by using them? Therefore how great a folly it is in the instance of sacred language, where theological and scriptural matters are treated, to disregard the particular character of the subject matter to arrive at the sense on the basis of grammatical rules![84]

In any case, as Wittgenstein notes: "If you can accept the miracle that God became man, then all these [textual] difficulties are as nothing. For then it is impossible for me to say what form the record of such an event should take."[85]

Rhees notes that recognizing the text as the Word of God "is not *finding out something about them*—like discovering the date when they

---

[82] Rhees, *Rush Rhees on Religion and Philosophy*, 44.
[83] Sasse, *Scripture and the Church*, 171.
[84] Luther, *Luther's Works*, 2:15.
[85] M. O'C Drury, in *Recollections of Wittgenstein* "Conversations with Wittgenstein," ed. Rush Rhees (Oxford: Oxford University Press, 1984), 164–5.

were written down. It is to live by them. If I say, 'This is the word of God', that is a confession of faith."[86] Indeed, Wittgenstein notes: "The historical accounts of the Gospels might, historically speaking, be demonstrably false and yet belief would lose nothing by this: *not*, however, because it concerns 'universal truths of reason'! Rather, because historical proof (the historical proof-game) is irrelevant to belief. This message (the Gospels) is seized on by me believingly (i.e. lovingly). *That* is the certainty characterizing this particular acceptance-as-true, not something *else*."[87] Moreover, he says: "*Here you have a narrative, don't take the same attitude to it as you take to other historical narratives!* Make a *quite different* place in your life for it."[88]

Just as there is a community who provided an account of the Word in language, and this account changes through time, there is also a change in the understanding of physics through time. In the case of the Judeo-Christian tradition, what is to be made of the understanding of God through this change? Is the data to be discarded? Rhees notes:

> Within a single tradition. Like that of the Hebrew religion, it can be said that the author of the second half of Isaiah meant the same by "God" as the author (or authors) of Genesis did, and that St. Paul meant the same by "God" as both of them because of the continuity of Hebrew worship and the kind of worship that was, the importance of such conceptions as "the God of our fathers", "the God of Abraham and the God of Jacob", and so on. But for Paul the same God could be worshipped by gentiles who were not the seed of Abraham and Jacob. And if gentiles worship the same God, then this must appear in what they say about God, in the way they worship and in what it means to them to be creatures and children of God. To ask "Do they worship the same God or not?" is to ask about that.[89]

---

[86] Rhees, *Rush Rhees on Religion and Philosophy*, 198.
[87] Wittgenstein, *Culture and Value*, 32.
[88] Ibid.
[89] Rhees, *Rush Rhees on Religion and Philosophy*, 46–7.

Did God change? Did the earlier communities get it wrong? No, instead this shows the essential aspect of the participatory relationship. Likewise, given the shift in physics from the classical, this is a consequence of a greater participatory role of the physicists. Moreover, our current conceptions can only be understood in the light of the former conceptions.

Realists in science and in religion constantly seek "something" beyond the given, beyond the measurements to hidden variables, beyond the random to determinism, beyond religious practices to the hidden God, beyond communities to an external authority, and beyond language to either an internal (mind) or an external foundation. In all these cases, what is "beyond" the realists is the fly-bottle's exit.

5

Conclusion

Realist debates between science and religion generate the largest volume of literature on the subject and appear to be the most stirring. The atheistic scientist in the vein of scientism happily shows the superiority of science over religion, which is not surprising since this scientist does nothing other than show that religion fails to meet his or her scientific standards. Is science superior? Well, if you want to investigate atomic structure, then yes. On the other hand, theologians may think that the scientist's principles are the intellectual standard so they enter this mode of reasoning and end up with a confused game. The unshakable consequence is a battle of flies working out a multitude of theories in a fly-bottle. Science and religion are continually caught in the gravity of realism and determinism from which many find it hard to escape—despite the potential exit provided by Wittgenstein and quantum theory—as understood by Bohr.

Rhees says: "We have grown up in a way of thinking about things and about men and about human affairs which makes it very difficult to turn to a religious way of thinking about them. This is not a matter of conflicting evidence. It is a matter of being able to think in this way at all."[1] There is no conflict *between* religion and science; rather, there is the confusion of realism *in* science and religion. We usually grow up in the realist's fly-bottle, which then furthers the problems and confusions of thinking we have *one* language and *one* grammar that explain an external and independent reality. Moreover, since this way of viewing things is so ingrained it leads many to think that the only possible

[1] Rhees, *Rush Rhees on Religion and Philosophy*, 202.

alternative to realism is nonrealism; yet nonrealism, once again, is stuck in the same bottle. To finally see the fly-bottle and its exit is not simply a matter of thinking with greater complexity; instead, as previously noted by Wittgenstein, it is getting over a certain resistance of one's will—it is easier to stay with the flies. Moreover, the seemingly exciting action of the flies continually flickering about, once stopped, seems void.

It should be apparent, once again, that scientism and reformed epistemology are really two sides of the same coin. Although these common debates between science and religion may seem invigorating and emotive for some, arguments within scientism are often nothing more than building a religious "straw man," showing that religion is senseless (compared to one's own scientism), and then burning it. This makes about as much sense as an illiterate recluse critiquing calligraphy as categorically senseless because it is senseless for him or her. The rejection of religion is not an empirical conclusion; it is an a priori rejection of religion. Moreover, the religious person does not offer a competing theory to a scientific theory for the best explanation of reality. It is not an issue in epistemology or a hypothesis; instead, it is a matter of logic understood at its depth—not as principles.

All too often theologians also attempt to find a realist foundation, whether it is an innate—God-given—ability of reason, a revealed text, or whatever; while in contrast the language and relational form of life of a religious community are regarded as secondary by-products. That is, there is a hope that they refer to the external foundational reality, but it is the form of life in the language matrix that is reality! Reality is neither a foundational structure with us living on top of it, nor is it a perfect reality "above" us; instead, reality is present and based on language, and the grammar of language is the limit of epistemology. It is dynamic and fluid—the stream of life—where what "is" cannot be understood as a logical necessity since language can change and randomness is built into the system.

If we try to fully explain this randomness then we miss it. Randomness, by nature, cannot be explained and if we could explain it then it would no longer have the importance it does. We cannot get outside reality since it is our reality, not under it or above it; just as we cannot step out of our thoughts to explain them. Neither science nor religion explain *everything*. Instead, quantum theory describes nature and religion describes a form of life, and the logic of this is seen in the language we use to state it as information—there is no external foundational template to which language and our concepts connect.

The logic and grammar that form propositions are our reality, and to reject it is not making a mistake, it would be a sign, within that particular community of not being able to make a mistake. Bohr notes the potential for divergent areas of study to meet on the basis of "logical character," namely, "the recognition of an analogy in the purely logical character of the problems which present themselves in so widely separated fields of human interest ... gives us an incitation to examine whether the straightforward solution of the unexpected paradoxes met with in the application of our simplest concepts to atomic phenomena might not help us to clarify conceptual difficulties in other domains of experience."[2] The point here is not to argue for or against science or religion, or to show that they are similar in realist terms and therefore, since religion is like science, it is acceptable. No. Religion is not a science. Yet there is a similarity between quantum theory as understood by Bohr and religion, namely, they both find meaning in their respective language matrix—which relationally forms information and reality.

Once realism is seen as a confusion, then the stereotypical debates between science and religion lose their importance. Humanity is much more complex than simply entering the correct program (education) into our brains—or through evolution eventually progressing

---

[2] Bohr, *Essays 1932–1957 on Atomic Physics and Human Knowledge*, Vol. II, 20.

beyond the "religion" gene—and then getting the true output. Indeed, the quantum itself evades any such deterministic systems. Also, what is missed is our relational character, value, and other features of life in contrast to basic scientific facts. The latter need not be "owned" by the person; indeed, not even related to or experienced by the person. A current science text describes certain facts and we generally agree with the basic facts. However, as Wittgenstein notes: "You cannot lead people to what is good; you can only lead them to some place or another. The good is outside the space of facts."[3] The flies cannot be led to the fly-bottle's exit by facts alone or mathematical structures; instead, like the good, it is discovered in the language nexus of information that is holistic and participatory. Once the exit is seen, one does not actually need to fly toward it since the bottle itself dissolves.

[3] Wittgenstein, *Culture and Value*, 3.

Bibliography

Atkins, Peter W. "The Limitless Power of Science," in *Nature's Imagination: The Frontiers of Scientific Vision*. Edited by John Cornwell. Oxford: Oxford University Press, 1995.

Baggot, Jim. *The Quantum Story: A History in 40 Moments*. Oxford: Oxford University Press, 2011.

Belfer, Israel. "Jacob Bekenstein and the Informational Turn in Theoretical Physics." *Physics in Perspective*, 16 (2014), 69–97.

Berkeley, George. *A Treatise Concerning the Principles of Human Knowledge*. Edited with an introduction by G. J. Warnock. La Salle, IL: Open Court, 1962.

Berstein, Richard. *Beyond Objectivism and Relativism: Science, Hermeneutics, and Praxis*. Philadelphia: University of Pennsylvania Press, 1983.

Bohr, Niels. "Causality and Complementarity." *Philosophy of Science*, 4, no. 3 (1937), 289–98.

Bohr, Niels. Collected Works, 13 volumes. General editor: Erik Rüdinger (–1989); Finn Aaserud (1989–). Amsterdam: North-Holland, 1972.

Bohr, Niels. "On the Notions of Causality and Complementarity." *Science*, 111, no. 2873 (1950), 51–4.

Born, Max. *Natural Philosophy of Cause and Chance*. Oxford: Clarendon Press, 1949.

Brukner, Äaslav, and Anton Zeilinger. "Information Invariance and Quantum Probabilities." *Foundations of Physics*, 39, no. 7 (2009), 677–89.

Calvin, John. *Institutes of the Christian Religion*. Translated by Henry Beveridge. London: Arnold Hatfield, 1959.

Carroll, Sean M. *From Eternity to Here: The Quest for the Ultimate Theory of Time*. New York: Dutton, 2016.

Dauben, Joeseph. *Georg Cantor: His Mathematics and Philosophy of the Infinite*. Princeton, NJ: Princeton University Press, 1990.

Davies, Paul. "Universe from Bit," in *Information and the Nature of Reality: From Physics to Metaphysics*. Edited by Paul Davies and

Niels Henrik Gregersen, 65–91. Cambridge: Cambridge University Press, 2010.

Davies, Paul, and John Gribbin. *The Matter Myth: Dramatic Discoveries That Challenge Our Understanding of Physical Reality*. New York: Simon & Schuster Paperbacks, 1992.

Dawkins, Richard. "Is Science a Religion?" *The Humanist* (Jan.–Feb. 1997), 26–39.

Descartes, René. *The Philosophical Writings of Descartes*. Translated by J. Cottingham, R. Stoothoff, and D. Murdoch. Cambridge: Cambridge University Press, 1985.

Dilman, İlham. *Philosophy as Criticism: Essays on Dennett, Searle, Foot, Davidson, Nozick*. Edited by Brian Davies and Mario von der Ruhr. New York: Continuum, 2011.

Dilman, İlham. *Wittgenstein's Copernican Revolution*. New York: Palgrave, 2002.

Dixion, Thomas. *Science and Religion: A Very Short Introduction*. Oxford: Oxford University Press, 2008.

Engelmann, Paul. *Letters from Ludwig Wittgenstein, with a Memoir*. Edited by B. F. McGuiness. Translated by L. Furtmuller. Oxford: Basil Blackwell, 1967.

Feynman, Richard P. *What Do You Care What Other People Think? Further Adventures of a Curious Character*. New York: W. W. Norton, 1988.

Harrison, Peter. *The Cambridge Companion to Science and Religion*. Edited by Peter Harrison. Cambridge: Cambridge University Press, 2010.

Heisenberg, Werner. *Physics and Beyond: Encounters and Conversations*. Translated by Arnold J. Pomeranz. New York: Harper & Row, 1971.

Heisenberg, Werner. *Tradition in Science*. New York: Seabury Press, 1983.

Heisenberg, Werner, Max Born, Erwin Schrodinger, and Pierre Auger. *On Modern Physics*. New York: Clarkson N. Potter, 1961.

Holmer, Paul. *The Grammar of Faith*. San Francisco, CA: Harper & Row, 1978.

Honner, John, and Niels Bohr. *The Description of Nature: Niels Bohr and the Philosophy of Quantum Physics*. Oxford: Oxford University Press, 1987.

Hustwit, Ronald E. *Something about O. K. Bouwsma*. New York: University Press of America, 1992.

Kant, Immanuel. *Critique of Pure Reason*. Translated by Werner S. Pluhar. Introduction by Patricia W. Kitcher. Indianapolis: Hackett, 1996.

Kerr, Fergus. *Work on Oneself: Wittgenstein's Philosophical Psychology.* The Institute for the Psychological Sciences Monograph Series, Vol. 1. Arlington, VA: Institute for the Psychological Sciences Press, 2008.

Kierkegaard, Søren. *Concluding Unscientific Postscript.* Translated by David Swenson, completed after his death. Introduction and notes by Walter Lowrie. Princeton, NJ: Princeton University Press, 1974.

Kierkegaard, Søren. *Soren Kierkegaard's Journals and Papers.* Edited and translated by Howard V. Hong and Edna H. Hong, assisted by Gregor Malantschuk. Vol. 3. Bloomington and London: Indiana University Press, 1975.

Lennox, John C. *God's Undertaker: Has Science Buried God?* Oxford: Lion Hudson, 2009.

Lennox, John C. *God and Stephen Hawking: Whose Design Is It Anyway?* Oxford: Lion Hudson, 2011.

Locke, John. *An Essay Concerning Human Understanding.* Edited with a foreword by Peter H. Nidditch. Oxford: Clarendon Press, 1985.

Luther, Martin. *Luther's Works: American Edition,* 55 volumes. Edited by Jaroslav Pelikan and Helmut T. Lehmann. St. Louis: Concordia; Minneapolis: Augsburg Fortress Press, 1955–1986.

Malcolm, Norman. "The Groundlessness of Belief." *Thought and Knowledge.* Ithaca, NY: Cornell University Press, 1977.

Malcolm, Norman. *Nothing Is Hidden: Wittgenstein's Criticism of His Early Thought.* New York: Basil Blackwell, 1986.

Malcolm, Norman. *Wittgenstein: A Religious Point of View?* Edited by Peter Winch. New York: Cornell University Press, 1995.

McGrath, Alister. *The Foundations of Dialogue in Science and Religion.* Oxford: Blackwell, 1998.

Monk, Ray. *Ludwig Wittgenstein: The Duty of Genius.* London: Jonathan Cape, 1990.

Moore, Andrew. *Realism and Christian Faith: God, Grammar, and Meaning.* Cambridge: Cambridge University Press, 2003.

Pais, Abraham. *Subtle Is the Lord: The Science and the Life of Albert Einstein.* Oxford: Oxford University Press, 2005.

Paparella, Emanuel L. *Hermeneutics in the Philosophy of Giambattista Vico: Vico's Paradox; Revolutionary Humanistic Vision for the New Age.* San Francisco: EMText, 2003.

Penrose, Roger. *Shadows of the Mind: A Search for the Missing Science of Consciousness*. Oxford: Oxford University Press, 1994.

Petersen, A. "The Philosophy of Niels Bohr," in *A Centenary Volume*, Part 6. Edited by A. P. French and P. I. Kennedy. Cambridge: Harvard University Press, 1985.

Phillips, D. Z. "Afterword," in *Wittgenstein's On Certainty: There—Like Our Life*. Edited by D. Z. Phillips, 133–82. Oxford: Blackwell, 2005.

Phillips, D. Z. *Wittgenstein and Religion*. Swansea Studies in Philosophy. Basingstoke: Macmillan, 1993.

Plotnitsky, Arkady. "Mysteries without Mysticism and Correlations without Correlata: On Quantum Knowledge and Knowledge in General." *Foundations of Physics*, 33, no. 11 (2003), 1649–89.

Polkinghorne, J. C. *Quantum Theory: A Very Short Introduction*. Oxford: Oxford University Press, 2002.

Polkinghorne, J. C. *Science and the Trinity: The Christian Encounter with Reality*. New Haven, CT: Yale University Press, 2004.

Rhees, Rush. *In Dialogue with the Greeks, Volume I: The Presocratics and Reality*. Edited by D. Z. Phillips. Burlington, VT: Ashgate, 2004.

Rhees, Rush. "Religion and Language." *Without Answers*. London: Routledge & Kegan Paul, 1969.

Rhees, Rush. *Rush Rhees on Religion and Philosophy*. Edited by D. Z. Phillips and Mario Von der Ruhr. Cambridge: Cambridge University Press, 1997.

Rhees, Rush. *Wittgenstein and the Possibility of Discourse*. Edited by D. Z. Phillips. Cambridge, England: Cambridge University Press, 1998.

Rosenfeld, Léon. "Niels Bohr's Contribution to Epistemology." *Physics Today*, 16 (Oct. 1963), 47.

Russell, Bertrand. *The Basic Writings of Bertrand Russell*. Edited by E. Egner and Lester E. Dennon. New York: Routledge, 2009.

Russell, Bertrand. *Introduction to Mathematical Philosophy*. Russell House: Spokesman, 1982.

Sasse, Hermann. *Scripture and the Church: Selected Essays of Hermann Sasse*. Concordia Seminary Monograph Series, Number 2. Edited by Jeffrey J. Kloha and Ronald R. Feuerhahn. Chelsea, MI: Book Crafters, 1995.

Sasse, Hermann. *We Confess Jesus Christ*. Translated by Norman Nagel. St. Louis: Concordia, 1984.

Shanker, S. G. *Wittgenstein and the Turning-Point in the Philosophy of Mathematics*. Albany: State University of New York Press, 1987.

Stapp, Henry. "Minds and Values in the Quantum Universe," in *Information and the Nature of Reality: From Physics to Metaphysics*. Edited by Paul Davies and Niels Henrik Gregersen, 104–20. Cambridge: Cambridge University Press, 2010.

Stenholm, Stig. *The Quest for Reality: Bohr and Wittgenstein; Two Complementary Views*. Oxford: Oxford University Press, 2011.

Stillman, Drake. *Discoveries and Opinions of Galileo*. New York: Doubleday-Anchor, 1957.

Tegmark, Max. *Our Mathematical Universe: My Quest for the Ultimate Nature of Reality*. New York: Knopf, 2014.

Vanhoozer, Kevin. *The Drama of Doctrine: A Canonical-Linguistic Approach to Christian Theology*. Louisville, KY: Westminster John Knox Press, 2005.

Wheeler, John. "The Computer and the Universe." *International Journal of Theoretical Physics*, 21, nos. 6–7 (1982), 557–72.

Wheeler, John. *Geons, Black Holes and Quantum Foam: A Life in Physics*. New York: Norton, 1999.

Wheeler, John. "Information, Physics, Quantum: The Search for Links." Proceedings from the 3rd International Symposium on Foundations of Quantum Mechanics, Tokyo, 1989.

Winch, Peter. *Ethics and Action*. London: Routledge & Kegan Paul, 1972.

Winch, Peter. *The Idea of a Social Science*. London: Routledge & Kegan Paul, 1958.

Wittgenstein, Ludwig. *The Blue and Brown Books*. Oxford: Basil Blackwell, 1972.

Wittgenstein, Ludwig. *Culture and Value*. Edited by G. H. von Wright in collaboration with Heikki Nyman. Translated by Peter Winch. Chicago, IL: Univeristy of Chicago Press, 1984.

Wittgenstein, Ludwig. *Notebooks*. Edited by G. H. von Wright and G. E. M. Anscombe. Translated by G. E. M. Anscombe. Oxford: Blackwell, 1979.

Wittgenstein, Ludwig. *On Certainty*. Edited by G. E. M. Anscombe and G. H. von Wright. Translated by Denis Paul and G. E. M. Anscombe. Oxford: Basil Blackwell, 1979.

Wittgenstein, Ludwig. *Philosophical Grammar*. Edited by Rush Rhees. Translated by Anthony Kenny. Oxford: Basil Blackwell, 1974.

Wittgenstein, Ludwig. *Philosophical Investigations*. Translated by G. E. M. Anscombe. Oxford: Basil Blackwell, 1988.

Wittgenstein, Ludwig. *Philosophical Remarks*. Edited by Rush Rhees. Translated by Raymond Hargreaves and Roger White. Oxford: Basil Blackwell, 1975.

Wittgenstein, Ludwig. *Remarks on the Foundations of Mathematics*. Edited by G. H. von Wright, Rush Rhees, and G. E. M. Anscombe. Translated by G. E. M. Anscombe. Oxford: Basil Blackwell, 1978.

Wittgenstein, Ludwig. "Sections 86–93 (pp. 405–35) of the So-Called 'Big Typescript.'" Edited by Heikki Nyman. Translated by C. G. Luckhardt and M. A. E. Aue. *Synthese*, 87, no. 1 (Apr. 1991), 3–22.

Wittgenstein, Ludwig. *Tractatus Logico-Philosophicus*. Translated by Raymond Hargreaves and Roger White. London: Routledge & Kegan Paul, 1986.

Wittgenstein, Ludwig. *Wittgenstein's Lectures, 1933–35: From the Notes of Alice Ambrose and Margaret Macdonald*. Edited by Alice Ambrose. Chicago, IL: University of Chicago Press, 1989.

Wittgenstein, Ludwig. *Wittgenstein's Lectures on the Foundations of Mathematics*. From the notes of R. G. Bosanquet, Norman Malcolm, Rush Rhees, and Yorick Smythies. Edited by Cora Diamond. New York: Cornell University Press, 1976.

Wittgenstein, Ludwig. *Zettel*. Edited by G. E. M. Anscombe and G. H. von Wright. Translated by G. E. M. Anscombe. Oxford: Basil Blackwell, 1967.

Wittgenstein, Ludwig, and Rush Rhees. "Wittgenstein's Philosophical Conversations with Rush Rhees (1939–50): From the Notes of Rush Rhees." Edited by Gabriel Citron. *Mind*, 124, no. 493 (2015), 1–71.

Zeilinger, Anton. "A Foundational Principle for Quantum Mechanics." *Foundations of Physics*, 29, no. 4 (1999).

Zeilinger, Anton. "The Message of the Quantum." *Nature*, 438, no. 7069 (2005), 743.

Zeilinger, Anton. "The Quantum Centennial." *Nature*, 408 (Dec. 2000), 641.

Index

a priori 24, 26, 38, 49–50, 52, 61, 77–9, 83–4, 87, 107
absolute the 53, 79
arbitrary 20, 26, 28, 30, 64, 66, 73, 85, 98–9, 106–7, 109, 120
Aristotle 61–3, 65, 70
atheist 3, 6, 91–2, 96, 116, 125
Atkins, Peter 3, 32
Atomism 18, 24, 34, 40, 47, 100

Baggot, Jim 13
Bekenstein, Jacob 80, 129
Berkeley, George 15, 18, 20, 22, 24, 68, 81, 129
Bernstein, Richard 74
body, the 17
Bohr, Niels
　complementarity 55–6, 60, 64, 116, 119
　correspondence principle 53
　language 50, 53–5, 66
　mathematics 43, 46, 52–3, 74, 86
　participatory information 54, 76
Boltzmann, Ludwig 23, 77–8, 88

calculations 35, 66–7, 70, 99, 103, 107, 110
Calvin, John 96
Carrol, Sean 9
Cartesian 19, 32, 61, 74, 111
Cartwright, Nancy 50
causality 1, 11, 58–61, 63–5, 67, 73, 78, 91, 107
classical physics 1, 8, 9, 11, 14, 22, 47, 52–3, 55, 58, 65, 70, 76, 84, 86, 93, 96, 98
classical theism 57 n.40, 107, 119
concepts and conceptual
　understanding 4, 6, 7, 12, 34–5, 39, 43, 45–6, 51, 53–5, 58, 60, 62, 64, 67–89, 92–4, 98–100, 103, 106, 109–10, 116, 119, 121–3
constructivist, mathematical 41
Copenhagen interpretation 8–9, 49–50, 52, 56, 87, 110, 116, 119

Davies, Paul 6, 43–4, 57, 70
Dawkins, Richard 3–5
decoherence 57
Descartes 15–19, 24, 34, 74, 79, 96, 113
determinism 1, 8–9, 11, 60, 62, 67, 73, 87, 106, 123, 125
Dilman, İlham 28, 30, 81, 82, 85, 88, 92, 110
Dirac, Paul 4
Drury, M. O'C. 68, 115

Einstein, Albert 35, 37, 58, 64, 69–71, 74, 94, 107, 118
empirical 7, 10, 37–8, 40–3, 47, 52–3, 63–7, 71, 73, 77, 85–6, 88–9, 95–6, 103–4, 110, 121, 126
empiricism, empiricist 19–20, 22, 32, 67, 78, 94, 96
epistemological, epistemology 10, 16–17, 28–9, 31–2, 36–9, 41–3, 46, 48, 52–3, 62, 69, 74, 86, 91, 96–8, 108, 110–11, 116, 118, 121, 126
Euclid, Euclidean 15, 36–8, 64, 88, 90, 120
Everett, Hugh 86
evidence 6, 53, 60–5, 91, 94–6, 98–9, 125
evidentalism 95–6
explanations 3–4, 67–8, 92, 111
external reality, world 2, 16, 18–20, 22–3, 25, 29, 31–2, 47, 49, 51, 54, 74, 77, 80

Feynman, Richard 72, 79, 101
form of life 14, 26–7, 29–30, 40, 42, 47, 49, 66–7, 71–2, 78, 88, 94, 97–8, 105–8, 120–1, 126–7
formalism, mathematical 8, 32, 40, 42, 46–7, 56
foundations 9, 11–12, 24, 28, 40, 68, 106
fundamentalism 2–3, 5–8, 98

Galileo 7, 43
geometry 15, 36, 38, 44, 64, 65
God
   in a form of life 106, 112, 114, 116, 119
   as foundation 34, 68, 96
   god of the gap 4–5
   as mystery 108–9
   reality of 104–5
   as a theory 94–5
Grib, A. A. 65

Hawking, Stephen 43
Hebblethwaite, Brian 93
Heisenberg, Werner 4, 7–8, 10, 12, 49, 51–2, 56, 67, 71, 74–6, 82, 116, 119
Hertz, Heinrich 54
hidden 58, 60, 69, 79, 93, 106, 111, 117–18, 123
Hilbert, David 32, 36, 43
Holmer, Paul 97, 99
Honner, John 13, 52–5, 61, 70, 72, 74–7, 80–1, 87
Huyssten, Wentzel van 93
hypothesis 28, 34, 66, 71, 93, 115–16, 126

idealism 17, 19, 32, 49, 77–8, 80–1
independent reality 19, 24, 28, 31, 38, 51, 58, 64, 81, 104, 125
information 8–9, 14, 57, 76, 78–80, 84, 86–7, 101, 103, 106, 109, 111, 114, 119, 127
intelligibility 71–2, 79, 83, 85, 117
irreducible 71, 106, 119

justification 32, 39, 41, 66, 97, 99, 111

Kant, Immanuel 76–80
Kerr, Fergus 77–8, 92, 95, 97, 99–100, 111–14, 116
Kierkegaard, Søren 46, 97, 109, 113, 116, 118
Kochen, Simon 65

language
   connection to reality, the world, and form of life 15, 20–2, 24–5, 27, 28–9, 51, 66, 78, 81–3, 85, 103, 105, 108, 110, 117, 126
   grammar 26–7, 30, 37, 40, 47, 55, 63, 65, 71, 84–5, 88–9, 98, 99–100, 102–5, 108–9, 125–7
   and logic 25, 27–8, 31, 50, 53, 57, 65, 73, 102, 118
   and mathematics 7, 10, 32–3, 35, 38–9, 44, 47, 49, 63, 65, 71–2
   ordinary 21–2, 52–4, 61, 65
   propositions 10, 21–7, 30–1, 35–42, 45–9, 52, 60, 62–5, 83–4, 86, 88, 94–6, 102–3, 105, 107–8, 127
language matrix 14, 82, 87–9, 91, 93–4, 98–9, 101, 108–9, 113–14, 119, 126–7
law(s) 6, 33, 36–7, 39, 43, 50, 56, 58–9, 63, 69–70, 75, 88, 93, 97
Lennox, John 3, 4, 7, 32, 117
Locke, John 15, 17–21, 24, 81, 95
logical atomism 34, 40, 47
logical syntax 22, 27, 31, 36–9, 43, 47, 50, 58, 60, 63, 65–6
Luther, Martin 112, 117, 121,

Malcolm, Norman 5, 6 n.10, 34–5, 99, 116
materialism 49–50, 74, 81
McGrath, Alister 115
measurement 9, 26, 41, 45, 51, 53, 56–8, 60–3, 65–6, 73, 85, 102–5, 110, 113, 118, 123

metaphysics, metaphysical 7–8, 10, 24, 28–30, 34, 41–2, 48, 50, 67–8, 77, 80, 97, 99–102, 106, 113
mind 17–20, 24, 49, 77–8, 80–2, 91, 94, 98, 113–14, 123
Monk, Ray 91
Moore, Andrew 94, 97, 98, 111
multiverse 6, 9, 45, 86, 101, 106, 108, 119
mystery 80, 106, 108–11, 118–19

Newton, Newtonian 33, 43, 50, 54, 58, 100
nonrealism 2, 11, 13, 15, 60, 67, 70, 91, 114, 126
numbers 8, 34–5, 39, 42, 47, 49, 95, 102

objective 1, 6, 36, 55, 61, 75–6, 82, 92–3, 96, 104, 109
observer 9, 15, 29–30, 47, 58, 60, 65, 69–71, 74–6, 79, 84–5, 101, 111, 113
ontology, ontological 30, 50, 62, 94, 120

Paparella, Emanuel 61
paradox 61, 65, 109–10, 119, 127
participatory 75–6, 114, 117–18, 123, 128
Pauli, Wolfgang 4, 58, 101
phenomena 44, 58, 60–1, 63–4, 66, 75, 78–80, 82, 93, 118
Phillips, D. Z. 10, 55, 71–2, 92, 98, 114
Plato, Platonic 21, 24, 34, 42, 47, 67, 84, 112, 115
Plotnitsky, Arkady 118
Polkinghorne, J. C. 9, 50, 56, 61f, 66–7, 71, 110f, 117
positivism, positivist 9, 11, 23, 25, 49
probability 56, 59, 69, 79, 85–6, 106, 108
Pythagoras 34

random 73, 106–7, 123, 126–7
realism

mathematics 10, 32, 34, 41, 47
philosophy 1, 2, 5–8, 13, 15–22, 24, 29–30
physics 11, 51–2, 57–8, 60–3, 67, 70, 75, 77–8, 80, 84
religion 91–3, 98, 101, 107, 111, 114–18
reductionism 32, 51, 86, 106
reformed epistemology 96, 111, 126
Rosenfield, Léon 54, 69
rule(s)
mathematics 32, 37–40, 42–4, 46–8, 72, 79
philosophy 25–6, 31, 103
physics 9, 53, 57, 60, 62–5, 85–7, 102, 104, 106–7, 110
religion 99, 121
Russell, Bertrand 26, 33, 73, 83, 91, 95

Sasse, Hermann 117, 120–1
Schrödinger, Erwin 9, 57, 107
Shanker, S. G. 32–3, 36, 38, 40, 42–6
skepticism 16, 19–20, 29, 31, 114
Soskice, Janet 94
space-time 69, 77–8, 85
statistical 8, 69, 86, 88–9, 102, 108
Stenholm, Stig 32, 40
subjective 61, 75–6, 82, 114
superposition 62–3
syntax 22, 27, 31, 36–9, 43, 46–7, 50–1, 58, 60, 63, 65–6, 86

Tegmark, Max 34–6, 45
true or false 10, 21, 24–6, 31, 36–7, 41, 47, 61, 62–5, 72, 84–6, 88, 103, 105, 107

Vanhoozer, Kevin 120
Vico, Giambattista 61

wave function 8, 63, 65, 89, 103, 106, 108
Wheeler, John 50, 53, 55–6, 75, 77, 79–80
Winch, Peter 25, 28, 39, 119
Wittgenstein, Ludwig

language-games 27–9, 31, 39, 55, 60, 63, 73, 82, 84, 87, 99, 100, 115
logic as shown in practice 25–31, 50, 52, 54–5, 58, 60, 66, 78, 81, 83–4, 107
logical form 21, 23–4, 26, 30–1, 39, 43, 47
mathematics 35–7, 39–42, 44, 47–8, 63, 65f, 86

religion 91, 95f, 104, 108, 113, 114–16, 121–2
underlying logical syntax 21–4, 31
Wolterstorff, Nicholas 120

Yukawa, Hideki 69–70

Zeilinger, Anton 12, 51, 55, 58, 62, 67, 73–4, 76, 79f, 83–4, 101, 106, 119
Zeno 37

www.ingramcontent.com/pod-product-compliance
Lightning Source LLC
Chambersburg PA
CBHW051813230426
43672CB00012B/2724